ONE
COMMUNITY

ONE
WEEK

MANY
FAITHS

The Diversity of
Worship and Belief

Edited by Eric Freedman and Howard Bossen

MICHIGAN STATE
UNIVERSITY

MICHIGAN STATE UNIVERSITY

For information, contact:

Michigan State University School of Journalism

404 Wilson Road

305 Communication Arts Building

East Lansing, Michigan 48824

Designed by Kenneth Villapando

Printed in the United States of America

Cover map used with permission of AAA Michigan

Library of Congress Cataloguing-in-Publication Data

ISBN 978-1-4951-3019-9

TABLE OF CONTENTS

TABLE OF CONTENTS

ACKNOWLEDGEMENTS

The enthusiastic participation of clergy and lay leaders from more than two dozen religious institutions was essential to this book, and we deeply appreciate their assistance. This project also couldn't have been possible without support from Dr. Lucinda Davenport, director of the MSU School of Journalism; Dr. Hiram Fitzgerald, associate provost for University Outreach and Engagement; and Paulette Granberry Russell, director of the Office for Inclusion and Intercultural Initiatives.

ONE
COMMUNITY
ONE
WEEK
MANY
FAITHS

Preface: The Various Roads We, as Humans, Travel

By the Very Reverend Sue Carter

I N THIS POST-MODERN world, we often hear the argument
that we live in a post-sacred world as well. After all, in April
1966—nearly a half century ago—didn't *Time* raise the question
of whether God is dead?

The Pew Research Center's Religion & Public Life Project
has studied and tracked American religious faith and practices
since 2001, examining the ways in which we express our faith.
In its 2007 in-depth research, the project revealed that, indeed,
more than a quarter of us have traded in our childhood faith
traditions for alternatives or abandoned them. Fully 16 percent
of people are completely unaffiliated, which is double the number
of people who had no church or temple or synagogue when they
were children. Those numbers have held steady for much of the
past decade.

In the chapters that follow, however, we borrow from Mark
Twain: the reports of God's death are exaggerated.

If religion is no longer the glue of American life, it certainly is a very strong and potent additive to it. For many, it defines the major events and the contours of our existence, from marriage and birth celebrations to death. Religion is central for many in the "match, hatch and dispatch" of who we are.

In the United States, unlike many other Western nations, religion plays a substantial role in our public lives as well. It is not surprising, then, that the Pew Research Center, which sees itself as nonpartisan and non-advocacy, has created a forum that looks at both religion and public life. In this land, the two have been joined in an unusual symbiosis for more than 400 years. The mix of religion and politics predates our national founding. One need be reminded only of the Pilgrims at Plymouth Rock to recall the role that religion has exerted in our nation's creation and operation.

While the meshing of religion into public life began prior to our nation's creation, it did not end there. Well before the U.S. Constitution was ratified and the country was established, Jesuits accompanied military expeditions led by France and Spain into this hemisphere. They joined explorers and soldiers in North America, venturing into the Midwest and beyond. Their immediate goal was to Christianize the native people. Their secondary goal was to negotiate contracts for land for political use.

The First Amendment to the U.S. Constitution is often cited for the proposition of a free press and free speech. Notably, though, the first freedoms in that amendment address religion: freedom from a state-established church and freedom to worship. In more contemporary times, religion and political—or public—life were ingredients of American society as the Silent Majority of Richard Nixon's presidency morphed into the Religious Right of Ronald Reagan's tenure.

Religion matters as part of the rich and complicated fabric of our nation.

It matters not only to people who practice a religion, but ironically also to those who do not. Otherwise, we would not have organizations of atheists or litigation over players' prayers before high school football games or Madalyn Murray O'Hair's Supreme Court case, which brought an end to public classroom prayer. Religion matters to soccer moms who ferry their children to Sunday morning games, but manage to get them shined up and in church for Easter. Religion matters to Jews who go to temple less frequently, but are present for High Holy Days. Religion matters to citizens and descendants of India, physically away from their heritage, who celebrate Diwali, Holi, Pongal and Dussehra. Religion matters for Muslims, native and foreign-born, who are at prayer on Fridays in the mosque and who strive to complete the hajj, the pilgrimage to Mecca.

As a priest, ordained in the Episcopal Church and part of the Anglican Communion, I am reminded that religion is not God. It is the human attempt to understand God in the many ways we experience a supreme being. Religion represents the various roads we, as humans, travel in striving to understand who we are relative to our creation and to our neighbors.

That is what this book addresses. It is about our community at worship in a wide range of religious traditions and about us as members of this "neighborhood" writ large. To quote Sesame Street, "These are the people in your neighborhood."

What a conglomeration our neighbors embody. In chapter two, Dr. K.S. Sripada Raju of the Bharatiya Temple in Haslett describes his understanding of God: "God is everywhere. God is in every form. God is in every being. So one has to develop a capacity and an attitude to recognize the presence of God."

The scope of faith Dr. Raju describes encompasses belief and practice—ways of understanding God and putting that faith into action. Practice includes the ritual and liturgy of Cristo Rey Roman Catholic Church in Lansing celebrating the Virgin of Guadalupe. In the nearby Islamic Center of East Lansing, it is the five daily services that begin with a call to prayer exalting God, the worshippers' belief and relationship with God and the recognition of Muhammad as God's messenger. The practice is a call for a peaceful Shabbat at Congregation Shaarey Zedek's Friday night service, less than three miles north of the Islamic Center. Members of Trinity African Methodist Episcopal Church put their faith into action with donations of furniture and lightly used clothing for Lansing residents, while at the same time paying attention to their own members and giving assistance where it is needed. At Discover Life Church, religious practice also becomes outreach. The people of the church spend time with residents of a low-income neighborhood in Lansing, sharing needed items and looking to spread their understanding of God.

These are but a few of the examples of religious life and worship in our community. The stories in this book try to capture the many approaches to belief and practice. The 2007 report from the Pew Research Center's Religion & Public Life Project listed as one of its findings that the "Midwest most closely resembles the religious makeup of the overall population" of the United States. The Greater Lansing area is in the heart of a Midwestern state. This book, this offering, represents then the diverse faces of our nation's people—who are working out their beliefs and living into relationships with others.

ONE COMMUNITY
ONE WEEK
MANY FAITHS

In the Beginning

By Eric Freedman

I N THE BEGINNING came the idea—three ideas, actually. First, teach a course about writing nonfiction books. Second, develop a collaborative project in which Michigan State University students would write a book together for publication. And third, choose a theme that would resonate with students and challenge them to think, write and get off campus and into the community.

If you're unfamiliar with the Lansing-East Lansing area, think of it as a tripod with three legs—the university, the state government and the automotive industry—that supports a major part of the economy and culture. Add in other higher education institutions, businesses, public and private schools, nonprofit organizations and local governments. Together they attract a wide array of people from across Michigan, from across the United States and from across the world. Some come here for only a year or two, some are students planning four-year stints and others stay longer, often permanently. In addition, many families have lived here for generations, maintaining an institutional memory of and for the community.

That's the "One Community" component of the project.

I mulled over potential book themes, ultimately choosing to focus on the role religious institutions and their worshippers play in a diverse, multi-faith and pluralistic community like ours. What aspects of faith unite—or divide—people? How do congregations—their clergy and lay leaders and their members—engage with the community at large? How do they promote and preserve their beliefs? How do they become part of the fabric of this community? Students would explore these and other questions by attending worship services, examining histories and missions, and interviewing clergy and lay members. They also would observe buildings, settings, people, music, words and activities.

That's the "Many Faiths" component of the project.

Members of my experimental "Writing the Nonfiction Book" course—a mix of undergraduate and graduate students—varied widely in their own religious practices and knowledge. For example, one had made a Christian mission trip to Central America, one was wrestling with a profound loss of faith and one had never been to any denomination's religious services other than funerals.

A week before the semester began, one student dropped the course after learning that this collaborative project would be a major part of the class. In an email, she wrote: "Based on the religious focus of the class project, I will withdraw. As an atheist, I am not willing to attend services. I also find the tentative title of the book problematic, as it implies that only people of faith are members of the community of East Lansing/MSU." Here's my reply:

> *I'm sorry to lose you, but I understand your decision. From my perspective, the religious beliefs or non-beliefs of a scholar or journalist for a research or journalism project are irrelevant. As writers and scholars, we often observe, learn about, interview and communicate about ideas, behaviors, people and practices that we're uncomfortable with or personally find distasteful. Our responsibility is to analyze and communicate, not to judge or vouch for what those people do or profess. We are not missionaries, proselytizers or evangelicals—nor are we skeptics, debunkers or underminers of any faith or denomination.*
>
> *Nor does the project imply that only people of faith—or the subset of those believers with a religious institution—are members of this community. Rather, they are among the many components of a broad tapestry of human beings who share a geographic space and choose their own way of engaging with their neighbors.*

To me, this student's withdrawal was an unfortunate, even tragic, missed opportunity. I believe that knowledge is power, and there was so much she could have learned about the community and about herself—and so much she lost by foregoing that experience. The situation reminds me of something Steven Greenebaum wrote in his book, *The Interfaith Alternative: Embracing Spiritual Diversity* (New Society Publishers, 2012): "The spiritual core of the universe has many voices, and indeed one of those voices is that of the Atheist. Let us rejoice in those many and profound voices *and then join together to build a world worth living in.*" Greenebaum also wrote, "All of us recognize that it is not how we encounter the sacred, but what we DO about it that counts."

My faculty colleague and this book's photography editor, Howard Bossen, a professor of visual journalism, organized a separate course so photojournalism students could participate in the project by teaming up with my writers. Sue Carter, another colleague who is both a journalism professor and an Episcopal priest, wrote the deeply moving essay on faith and diversity that precedes this introduction.

For the project, I assigned each writer three religious institutions to visit and profile. I required them to attend at least one worship service at each institution during a mid-October 2013 stretch of two weekends and the days in between, although we bent the time rules a bit for logistical reasons.

That's the "One Week" component of the project.

But which institutions should we visit? I started with the Yellow Pages, which included about 400 local listings under "churches" plus two synagogues and one mosque. Some were in inner-city neighborhoods, some were within sight of campus and some were in nearby suburbs. I received recommendations and searched the Internet for faiths that lacked Yellow Pages listings. For a maximum diversity of faiths, I usually chose only one, rarely two, of the same denomination and emailed or phoned the lead clergy or a lay leader to explain the project and seek their cooperation. Most agreed to participate, but a few declined and some did not respond. Thus this book doesn't claim to be encyclopedic, but instead is representative of the wide variety of faiths in our community.

And how to assign students? To stretch their experiences, one guiding principle was to not assign a writer to a denomination he or she belonged to or had grown up in. The rest of the assignment process was largely calendar-driven; for example, I couldn't assign a student to three churches that held their only weekly worship at 10 a.m. on Sundays.

After returning from her three assigned religious institutions, one student who belongs to a mainstream Christian denomination described the experience as going beyond her comfort zone and feeling herself in the minority. To me, that's a sign of the project's success.

1

Adventism Is a Way of Life
— Bethel Seventh-day Adventist Church, Lansing

By Katlin Barth with photography by Breanna Bishop

O N THIS SATURDAY in mid-October, the Lansing Bethel Seventh-day Adventist Church fills its sanctuary with more songs than members. The welcoming service is filled with singing, piano tunes and drumbeats. On average, seventy to 100 members attend Saturday worship services, but today's attendance is smaller because the youth group is on a weekend camping trip.

Before leading another song of praise, the head of the three-woman choir says, "We came to hear God talk to us through His music." Head Elder Gerard Mauzé explains that music is an important and complementary aspect of their worship and brings worshippers to a heaven-like state that gives them a clear space to think about what's being preached. He cautions that the music should be good enough to lift people into that state of mind but not so emotional that they forget to consciously think.

9

Saxophonist Kosly Joseph performs a song of meditation.

Elder Mauzé leads today's service since Pastor Harold Allison is preaching at a church in Jackson where he is also the pastor.

Later, Pastor Allison explains his belief that music is one of the three main aspects of a Seventh-day Adventist service. To him, preaching is the message of God, prayer is a petition to God and music is a testimony to God. "Music is just as important as prayer and preaching. Music is an expression of the heart for what God has done."

Some Seventh-day Adventist churches play loud organ music and move worshippers through a series of standing and sitting positions. In others, worshippers are always standing and clapping. Pastor Allison says Lansing Bethel falls somewhere in the middle.

The congregation is predominately African American and is a mix of the elderly, university students and families with small children. Members take roles in the service. For example, three sing in the choir, one plays the piano and another accompanies the pianist on a drum set.

Another member invites the children to the front of the sanctuary for an interactive lesson. During this service, only two children sit on the steps of the pulpit. They are taught that God wants us to follow His voice. To demonstrate, Braxton, the older child, is asked to close his eyes and follow another member's voice as she moves around the church.

Diane Dalton, a lay pastor, leads the congregation in prayer and invites those who are willing and those who are able to join hands at the front of the sanctuary. More than half the congregants leave their seats to participate. Even those who have difficulty walking move to the front pew and share prayer with the others. Some members find the prayer so moving that they wipe away tears.

So far, the congregants have moved around the church, but when Elder Mauzé comes to the podium to preach, all twenty-nine worshippers sit and listen to his message. He looks the part of an elder. He has a salt-and-pepper-flecked beard and black-rimmed glasses, and he speaks to the congregation rather than at them. Worshippers often answer his open-ended questions or say "amen" when they agree with the preaching.

ELDER MAUZÉ AND other elders and guest speakers preach to the congregation when Pastor Allison is away. Elder Mauzé's responsibilities include living in the community and not only knowing the church's members but being close to them as well. Lansing Bethel has had many pastors throughout its history. Pastor Allison arrived in March 2013 and will leave when construction of a new church building is completed, which is expected to be next spring. Elder Mauzé says he is able to provide stability to the church even as the pastoral leadership changes.

This Saturday's lesson focuses on a healthy lifestyle, which is important to Seventh-day Adventists. Elder Mauzé speaks of balancing our lives with rest on the Sabbath. Work always follows us, and after he observes how we're always on our phones, his rings and he pauses mid-sermon to answer it. Members of the congregation laugh. He goes on to say that we need to learn when to engage and when to disengage. By saying yes to everything, we don't have time to eat or sleep properly, which pushes us to look toward substances like coffee, tobacco and energy drinks.

A common misconception is that Seventh-day Adventists are stuck up and believe they practice faith better than adherents of other religions, Elder Mauzé says. But they don't practice faith better than others, he says—they just practice it more strictly. Most Seventh-day Adventists tailor their work schedules, diets and habits to follow the guidelines of their religion. And Pastor Allison refers to their religion as more than just a set of beliefs: "Adventism is a way of life."

Sabbath, their day of worship and rest, lasts from Friday at sunset to Saturday at sunset, and adherents usually avoid work during that time. "Most employers will work out a schedule with them, and if not they will find another job because it's a lifestyle," says Pastor Allison.

Diet is another aspect that determines how Seventh-day Adventists live their lives. Forty percent of the congregation is vegetarian, while the rest practice a "clean meats" diet. The "clean meats" are determined by rules found in Leviticus 11 and Deuteronomy 14: Meat must be from a cud-chewing animal with split hooves, and fish must have fins and scales.

Seventh-day Adventists take care of their bodies because they believe that their bodies are the temples of God, so congregants are also expected not to use tobacco, drink alcohol or use drugs. Other aspects of Adventism include adopting a modest style of dress—for example, women wear little or no makeup or jewelry—and donating 10 percent of one's income plus giving freewill offerings to the church.

Because of these offerings, the increase in membership and the hard work of Pastor Allison and congregants, a new church is being built at the intersection of Jolly Road and Martin Luther King Jr. Boulevard in Lansing. Both Pastor Allison and Elder Mauzé hope the new building will give the church new ways to interact with the community. Even though he won't be there, Pastor Allison hopes everyone in the community will enjoy the new church.

"THE BIBLE TALKS about being the salt of the earth, a preservative, and if you're not making a social impact, then you're just occupying real estate," says Pastor Allison. The church can't be everything to everyone, but it can be something of importance to someone. He wants Lansing Bethel to be a place where children can get off the street for a few hours and where the elderly can play dominos. He and Elder Mauzé want the community to benefit from the building on more days of the week than just Saturdays.

"Jesus made us fishermen," says Elder Mauzé, who hopes to help community residents and church members lead healthier lifestyles with classes that focus on quitting smoking, transitioning to a better diet and managing their finances. Pastor Allison also hopes members will create a family life program where people with family problems can

Gabriel Greenidge is one of the church's young ushers. The church includes children's stories during services and youth programs.

find solutions. The new church should be a place where people feel welcomed and not judged, "a place where the single mother with four kids can come, or the gangbanger with saggy pants who's looking to turn his life around, or the recovering alcoholic can come and find support. That's where I expect to see them in the next five years."

ACCORDING TO THE church's beliefs, all of us are seekers looking for a place where we can find God. He keeps the doors open regardless of where you come from, what your background is or how you look. Those who already belong to Lansing Bethel are learning to accept new members, which has helped almost double the membership to 173. Members are realizing that visitors are where they themselves once were—on a journey. "Someone took time to help them along the way, and now they get the chance to help someone else," Pastor Allison says.

"At our church, faith is an experience and faith is a reality and faith is a journey. You're not expected to be a full-fledged Christian—you're only expected to grow as Christ leads. You don't have to know everything—just be willing to learn."

Practicing the Value of Truth

— Bharatiya Temple, Haslett

By Tyler Hendon with photography by Carra Oteto

"GOD IS EVERYWHERE. God is in every form. God is in every being. So one has to develop a capacity and attitude to recognize the presence of God," Dr. K.S. Sripada Raju tells a group of devotees at the Bharatiya Temple in Haslett. It is a Monday evening, and ten Hindus are gathered to pray and worship in unison. A few more people enter the temple as the service gets underway.

Hinduism is entrenched in universal values and a love for human life, Dr. Raju explains. "I'm stuck in practicing the value of truth, the value of harmony and the value of love. These concepts are what bring me to this temple every day, in one form or another. This temple is a place where we come to worship God and humble ourselves."

Originally from India, Dr. Raju's belief in unity and Hinduism has kept his spirits high during his time in the United States as a student and teacher. He has served as a Brahman—a

Inside the Bharatiya Temple

priest who keeps an eye out for possible errors during spiritual rituals—for the temple's ceremonies. A teacher of Hindu scriptures, he has been a part of Greater Lansing's Hindu community since 1990.

Original construction of the temple began in 1992 and finished in 1994. Hindus celebrated the temple's inauguration on Maha Shivaratri Day marking the annual festival held in reverence of Lord Shiva. Nearly 400 people gathered that day for the ceremony, a huge number compared to the average of ten to twenty worshippers who attend the temple's weekday services. Devoted citizens in the community pledged money toward the building project in an effort to have a spiritual home for the Hindu community.

BEFORE ENTERING THE sanctuary, visitors take off their shoes, and some even go as far as taking off their socks. A sign stating "Please help your God's house by keeping silence in sanctorum area" is at the front of the sanctuary. Red, orange and gold decorations rest in every corner of the building. Tasseled embroideries make the space bright. A glass chandelier hangs over the sanctuary. As the sanctuary doors swing open, light glistens off of the chandelier, exposing the room's bright, radiant colors as worshippers greet each other quietly. The carpeted floor allows for a comfortable place to sit while worshipping.

Within the sanctuary, a single candle burns on top of a large metal vase, and there are two wooden boxes for donations. One at a time, attendees quietly walk over to the box and insert dollar bills.

MUSIC ROOTED IN Indian tradition plays softly during the service. The priest, or *panditiji,* of the Bharatiya Temple is Srihari Kadambi. He explains, "Our music gives a sense of sharing, joy and helping each other. God has given to us; therefore, we will share and give it back to God. This is an important part of being Hindu people. I urge you all to give generously."

The temple offers spiritual classes for children and adults looking to grow closer to their faith. During these classes, adults can meet with spiritual leaders such as Dr. Raju and learn scriptures. Children are able to learn Hindi songs, attend Hindi movie nights and participate in celebratory potlucks. Panditji Kadambi says, "We help people that like to learn. Helping people is my livelihood."

He believes that Hinduism and its culture are open to anyone with an open mind. He also believes people of all religious denominations must be able to live amongst each other. "We must love each other and accept each other. Acceptance is a big part of loving those around you, regardless of the circumstance."

Upward, Inward and Outward

— Capital City Vineyard, East Lansing

By Marisa Hamel with photography by Erin Hampton

"WHAT I FIND is if you're really poor, there are services. If you make a really good income, you don't need it. It's the people who have jobs that are minimum wage but can't make ends meet at the end of the month." Standing in front of wire racks of deodorant, bar soap, tissues, toothpaste and other toiletries, Kathy Tobe waits for volunteers to help sort through the rest of the items next to a shelf of free children's books. "That's what I found when working with Christian Services—that there's really a need for the ones that fall through the cracks."

Tobe started the personal needs pantry for Capital City Vineyard. It's part of an association of contemporary evangelical churches known as the Vineyard that began in the 1970s in California. The Vineyard on Coolidge Road is a long, clean building surrounded by a green community garden and a new playground.

On the day of the annual Harvest Festival for Vineyard

Jonathan Alvaro plays the keyboard during worship services.

guests and other community residents, children slip down the slides and pump their legs on the swings. A cluster of adults grill burgers and hotdogs after the service. Until meeting Pastor Kevin Shoemaker, an outsider might wonder if this is even a church at all.

Most families who benefit from the Vineyard's personal needs pantry are low-income immigrants—nearly 60 percent Muslim—from the Pebble Creek Apartments across the street. Food stamps don't cover necessities like toiletries and kitchen supplies, so people can come in once a month to fill a bag with personal care items, all free of religious affiliation to the Vineyard. The pantry also collects leftover bread from Panera every Saturday night, and church volunteers personally hand them out door-to-door to Pebble Creek residents on Sunday afternoons.

"I'm really into meeting new people and this is just an icebreaker," Tobe says of the bread and personal needs pantry. "We do not push church on them; we just want to be loving to people."

And loving they are. The mission of the Vineyard is "deepening relationships upward, inward and outward." Pastor Shoemaker describes the pantry as an opportunity to extend physical and emotional nourishment to those who would not know where to look for it otherwise.

"What I hear most commonly is that people appreciate the warmth and welcoming atmosphere. We work hard at that. It's very deliberate. We don't want to be a closed or inward-focused group."

By giving away bread, congregants are also giving a symbol of God's love. He wants to love people where they are, whether that is a life transition like immigrating to a new country, a time of financial difficulty or even emotional struggle. That is where the pastor levels with most of the families at Pebble Creek. "We think of the services that would bless those people."

The ministry has grown to include tutoring programs for kindergarten through high school students twice a week, offered in collaboration with Michigan State University students. Shelves in the library overflow with donated collections of colorful picture books and thick theology books that are available for checkout and return on an honor system. For adults, English as a Second Language and citizenship classes are held in church classrooms.

During a Sunday morning service, Pastor Shoemaker asks congregants to step forward and volunteer "once a week or once a month" to help the visitors. He reaches out his hands and calls them the new generation of workers who will carry out ministry in the future. The purpose, he adds, is not to serve people who are saved by Christ. It is to bring Christ to the people who are without Him.

What we found, and this is biblical too, is that worship is of huge importance in the life of the church. It's our declaration and our expression of who God is, so we want that to be first priority in the kind of music that we sing and in the way we sing it.

—Pastor Kevin Shoemaker

AS PEOPLE WALK into a typical Vineyard worship service, two greeters hand out programs and point toward the Café, which offers coffee, tea and gluten-free cookies to snack on during the service. The main area buzzes with greetings as name tags are stuck on sweaters. "We don't want it to be like what people imagine in their minds as religion," Tobe says.

The Vineyard is an ethnically diverse and family-centered congregation of about 150 members, about one third of them children. Graduate students, singles, couples and families with children of all ages are drawn to the church, partly because of its informal worship style, but also because of its grounded focus on Scripture, prayer and service. The Vineyard moved to its current location ten years ago after branching off from another Vineyard in Holland, Michigan.

A noteworthy trait of the worship service is the upbeat, prayerful Christian music, which is often written and produced in local Vineyard churches and heard on Christian radio.

"They really love God. This is not a show. We're not going through the motions. This is life for us," Pastor Shoemaker says, observing that Scripture is the basis for giving practical life advice and encouragement.

Families worship together during the music and are blessed and dismissed for individual lessons in their age groups. The pastor's wife, Beth Ann Shoemaker, often teaches "Kid's Church" during the regular worship service to bring Scripture down to a level the younger members can understand. "I remember sitting bored to tears during church, thinking how long could an hour possibly last?" Pastor Shoemaker jokes about going to church as a kid.

The main sermon is directed toward adults, and many bring notebooks and sip coffee during his PowerPoint presentation.

Pastor Shoemaker became interested in ministry after he worked at a Christian summer camp during his college years. At the time, he was a business major, but now "the rewards are completely different. I'm not getting paid a lot of money and I'm not getting rich, but I love what I do."

The harvest is plentiful but the workers are few.
—Matthew 9:35

THIS PARTICULAR SUNDAY is the birthday of the Vineyard, and the celebration is a Harvest Festival. A potluck lunch steams on long banquet tables covered in mums and orange tablecloths, complete with pork-free dishes for Muslim families. Before forks hit the plates, a congregant approaches Pastor Shoemaker to ask him to bless the meal. He replies that anyone from the congregation can do it, but with one requirement. "My only thought is if anyone from Pebble Creek is here yet? I don't want our guests to show up and all the food's gone."

He talks about "evangelism" the way a hairdresser measures a trim—as second nature. He's not on the corner with a megaphone. Instead, he's talking with neighbors about their kids and busy schedules over a cup of joe. "I'm not trying to preach. I'm just trying to be real. This is what makes me tick, this is what fulfills my life," he says. "To me, that's what evangelism should be." One challenge in the church is getting people to be outward with their faith in a culture that has fallen away from religion. So the Vineyard provides members with many opportunities to practice their faith, such as attending the Harvest Festival, helping in classrooms or assisting with the pantry, tutoring services and library. They receive freely and give freely.

"We decided when we first began that one of the reasons why churches often have a negative reputation, like the television evangelists, is that they're always asking for money," Pastor Shoemaker remarks. "So we decided we're not going to ask for money."

Pastor Shoemaker says the church rarely asks the congregation for money. In the Jewish tradition from Scripture, offering plates are absent from the service so worshippers can focus on the Word of God, but offering boxes are available in the Café. The church operates solely on the devotion and gifts of its members, and when visitors come, they're offered coffee instead of solicited for a donation. "We're not trying to make a profit—we're trying to change people's lives."

He had compassion on them because they were harassed and helpless, like sheep without a shepherd.

—Matthew 9:36

A YEAR AND a half ago, a woman from Pebble Creek experienced a tragedy when her son was shot and killed in a robbery. The pastor remembers, "She didn't have a church, hadn't been to church, but because we had been to her apartment and built a relationship with her and she trusted us because we went every week to bring bread, and she asked me to do the funeral."

The funeral parlor was packed with more than 400 people. "It was a pretty rough crowd. Most of them were not churchgoers. But to me it was such a privilege to speak about this young man and our relationship with him through the church."

Pastor Shoemaker says if you see with the eyes of Jesus, you will feel with the heart of Jesus. The Sunday sermon references the Latin word for compassion, rachamin, which relates to touching the depth of a mother's womb or reaching a person's deepest needs. Referring to a passage from the Gospel of Matthew, he asks, what are sheep without a shepherd? The answer is that they're vulnerable, and inviting people to be like Jesus is to invite them to care for and protect the vulnerable.

OUTSIDE THE BUILDING is a community garden cared for by Farah Aslani, a Persian woman from Pebble Creek. This is her fifth year coordinating and allotting the thirty-two plots for people from Pebble Creek, Haslett and Okemos. They are each given a 10.5-by-11-foot plot to plant with fruits and vegetables, which are often representative of their home countries. The garden is as diverse as the gardeners. Families from South Africa, Saudi Arabia, Iran, France, Bosnia and Nigeria cultivate the fruits, vegetables and roots to cook in their homestyle dishes. Gardeners grow peppers, squash, watermelon, rosemary, cilantro, basil, cabbages, corn, broccoli, beans, okra, eggplant and even the Swiss chard that Aslani has seen tossed into salads or soups.

"Some of this food is just nostalgia," says Aslani, who has tasted a Nigerian ugu vegetable soup made by a neighbor whose husband had brought the seeds when he moved from Africa. There are two experimental plots, one of which grew peanuts for a resident whose mother was dying of cancer. Her mother wanted to taste fresh peanuts, reminiscent of what grew in her home country. Aslani describes the garden as a necessity for the community. The organic produce brings nutrients and a piece of home to the refugees and immigrants, and the Vineyard is happy to share the land.

"Freely you have received, and freely you shall give," Pastor Shoemaker says during the service. The gardeners often bring their extra fruits and vegetables to the Vineyard to share with the congregation. Aslani leaves bundles of fresh herbs and vegetables on cars for congregants to find after the service. The joy the Vineyard brings to the community—a bread pantry, a potluck lunch or a plot of dirt—tenderly pushes a diverse and vulnerable people a bit closer together so that they are not sheep without a shepherd.

"We have free water, free land and the money people give me I use for the garden." Aslani says. "The garden is my passion; it is my health."

Pastor Kevin Shoemaker talks about the history of Capital City Vineyard.

4

Shabbat Shalom –
A Peaceful Shabbat

— Congregation Shaarey Zedek, East Lansing

By Duygu Kanver with photography by Ashley Weigel

IT IS A quarter past 7 o'clock in the evening. On this chilly, rainy Friday night, few cars seem to be out on Coolidge Road, which is dark and nearly empty. On the right side of the road as drivers travel northbound, they see the huge shadow of a dark, intriguing sculpture reflected on the high, windowless walls of a brick building. Located in the center of a grassy lawn, the sculpture stands some fifty yards from the road, making it impossible for nighttime passers-by to tell what it depicts. While its appearance may give some the chills, others think it's a sublime image.

The building is Congregation Shaarey Zedek. And the dark, intriguing sculpture depicts two towers of abstract figures holding a big menorah, the seven-branch candelabra that is an ancient symbol of Judaism. In contrast with the dark and empty road, the synagogue is luminous and crowded inside.

IT IS FRIDAY evening, the beginning of Shabbat, the seventh day of the week and a day of rest for Jews. During Shabbat, which continues until sunset on Saturday, they observe their holy day with prayer, services and festive meals. People in small groups enter the synagogue through the back door near the parking lot—an interesting habit. Rabbi Amy Bigman smilingly says there is no rule telling people to do so, but no one uses the front door anyway.

A leaflet printed on purple paper is handed to the congregants as they enter. On the leaflet is the Torah reading of the week, announcements, the prayers to be sung in the service and a list of yahrtzeits, the names of congregants' loved ones whose anniversary of death is around that day. Before taking seats in the sanctuary to welcome the arrival of Shabbat, congregants greet each other in the hall by wishing "Shabbat Shalom," a peaceful Shabbat.

Tonight, the 230-seat capacity sanctuary has about 190 worshippers by Rabbi Bigman's estimate. Someone who visits Shaarey Zedek for the first time on this Friday would think it has a considerably large congregation, but they are gathered to celebrate two special events this day in addition to Shabbat. The first is Executive Director Patty Warshaw's tenth anniversary at Shaarey Zedek and the second is the aufruf, or blessing, of two young congregants, Adam and Ali, before their wedding. On this special evening, more than a hundred guests join the fifty congregants who usually attend Friday night services, making this Shabbat even more festive.

It is colorful inside the sanctuary. The bright colors of the women's elegant outfits, together with the men's blue, purple, silver-gray satin and crocheted kippot (skullcaps), balance the dominant brown of the wooden walls. On the walls are plaques with names, dates and small light bulbs. An orange light glows on some, while the lights are off on the majority of the others. These plaques memorialize congregants' loved ones, and the illuminated ones are those whose yahrtzeit is marked this week.

The bimah (pulpit), a few steps above the floor, is well-lit. Engraved on the wall in gilded Hebrew and English letters is a quote from Proverbs, one of the books of the Jewish Bible or Tanakh, about understanding the wisdom of Torah: "It is a tree of life to them that grasp it" (Proverbs 3:18). A jazz trio plays, and as a tribute to the special events of the day, Cantor Pamela Schiffer sings with the group. Her voice and hand movements, along with the vivid tunes performed by the trio, lift the spirits of the worshippers. "Whoa," a wedding guest says to a first-timer in the synagogue about the trio, "I come from Indiana, and I attend a Jewish Reform synagogue there as well, but it's nothing like this. This synagogue is the rock star of all synagogues."

Although pleased with the positive reaction she receives from the guests, Rabbi

The Torah

Rabbi Amy Bigman

Bigman says Shabbat services aren't always like this. Instead of a jazz trio, a pianist or a guitar player usually accompanies Cantor Schiffer on Friday nights. Cantor Schiffer, who is at Shaarey Zedek part-time, co-leads the Friday night service with the rabbi and leads Shabbat morning's Conservative service when she is in town. When the cantor is away, Rabbi Bigman and a soloist officiate on Friday night, while the rabbi officiates on Saturday.

During the Conservative service on Saturdays, no musical instrument is played, however. "It's all voice, and that's very traditional," says Rabbi Bigman. But without letting go of the tradition, the congregation makes sure to include music in the Friday services, particularly for special occasions like today's because, as the rabbi puts it, "If the words in the prayer book don't touch your heart, sometimes music can do it."

When it comes to touching the congregants' hearts, the musical contribution by Cantor Schiffer and the jazz trio is undeniable, but the prayers alone are also moving. English and Hebrew are in balance—every congregant, even non-Hebrew speakers, understands the content and experiences this ineffable feeling of holiness that comes with the short, tonic syllables of the Hebrew words of prayer. Hebrew is written from right to left, so the service may be a little hard for a first-timer to follow, not because of the foreign language, but because of the reverse order of the prayer book contrasted with books written in the Latin alphabet. What would be the last page in an English-language book is the first page here. Seeing that a guest couple is having a hard time finding the right page in *Mishkan T'filah*, the Reform siddur (prayer book), a congregant graciously helps them as the service continues.

The Friday service is usually short, but this day's is an exception. On a regular Friday night, prayers from *Mishkan T'filah* occupy most of the service. But today, celebrations of Adam and Ali's aufruf and Warshaw's tenth anniversary extend the service to almost two hours. Of course, witnessing all the joy, celebrating a young couple's marriage and seeing how members speak proudly of Warshaw as she smiles with tears on her face make these two hours well-spent. After the ceremonies, Rabbi Bigman explains that a two-hour service is usually the case on Saturdays but not on Fridays.

SATURDAY MORNING IS when congregants gather for the Conservative service. Not only is it longer than Friday night's, but it's also more formal. Traditionally, all men wear kippot on Saturdays, while it is optional for women. There is silent prayer, as well as the week's Torah reading in Hebrew. As the service is in Hebrew, for many guests "it is hard to follow," says Rabbi Bigman. "It was hard for me to follow when I first came here."

After services, congregants meet in the social hall for Oneg Shabbat (Joy of the Sabbath) on Friday night and Kiddush (Holiness or Sanctification) on Saturday morning. This night, homemade desserts, pastries and a chocolate cake to celebrate Warshaw's anniversary and the marriage of Adam and Ali are set on a long table in the middle of the room. Congregants take some of their favorites and sit at one of the eight round tables or stand in small groups and chat. Everyone is encouraged to eat before they leave. "To me, the meal that is shared is the most important part of Shabbat," Rabbi Bigman tells one guest.

SHAAREY ZEDEK'S SISTERHOOD is a group of members who volunteer in activities for the good of their synagogue, of Greater Lansing and of Jewish youth. On its website, the Sisterhood defines its main goal as "to invest in the future of our youth."

The rabbi thinks the same way; she emphasizes the importance of youth in their community and is happy that the congregation includes a good mix of ages. Thanks to its loca-

A memorial in the sanctuary for Jews killed in the Holocaust

tion in a college town, there are many young people among its 255 member families. And for Rabbi Bigman, a main goal is to keep engaging the children of these young families in the community. To achieve that, the focus is on education for all ages—the synagogue's youth education program starts from pre-kindergarten and goes through twelfth grade.

Rabbi Bigman emphasizes the value of educating children and youth: "Seeing a child start the school when he or she is very little and go all the way until the twelfth grade in Shaarey Zedek is the most rewarding feeling." There's an adult education program as well, and Rabbi Bigman emphasizes that the education of all people is valuable. "And so is helping people in their difficult times and helping them to celebrate their happy occasions."

Sculpture in front of
the synagogue

5

Primero Dios
— Cristo Rey Roman Catholic Church, Lansing

By Jordan Jennings with photography by Olivia Hill

W HO IS THE Virgin of Guadalupe? You may know her as
Mother Mary.

According to Hispanic Roman Catholicism, La Virgen
de Guadalupe appeared in a vision to a Mexican man named
Juan Diego in 1531. She appeared to Diego twice, asking him
to tell the Bishop to build her a church. Diego obeyed, but he
was refused twice by the Bishop. The third time Mother Mary
came to Diego, she instructed him to go into the desert to pick
roses and bring them to the Bishop. He collected the roses that
miraculously grew there and brought them in his robes to the
Bishop. When he pulled the roses out of his robe, both he and the
Bishop were shocked to see an image of La Virgen de Guadalupe
imprinted on the front of Diego's robe. After this supernatural
sign, the Bishop readily agreed to build a church.

Hispanic Catholics say the original image that appeared
on Diego's cloak is in the Basilica of Our Lady of Guadalupe in

Father Frederick Thelen walks toward the altar.

Mexico City, but a replica is located at the rear of Cristo Rey Roman Catholic Church's sanctuary. It is an elaborate image of the woman with her head bowed in prayer and a bow around her stomach symbolizing her sacred pregnancy. Lavish bouquets, candles and a place to kneel in prayer cover the floor before her. Reverend Fredrick Thelen explains that this is a place to ask the Lady to pray as an intercessor for us, and the candles are physical representations of prayers as they burn.

DOWNSTAIRS, AROUND A dozen church members stand in Cristo Rey's kitchen. They cook tortillas on skillets, scoop refried beans from a metal pot, sprinkle lettuce, dollop rice and plop guacamole onto paper plates. Volunteers pass the full plates through a large window where members wait excitedly. Father Thelen says it is these volunteers, as well as the janitors, who keep the church running.

Beside the window, a blackboard menu written in chalk reads, "MENU: 1 Gordita, Arroz y Frijoles Gorditas" with prices up to five dollars.

Teenager Julissa Rodriguez says this mouth-watering luncheon is a common event. Each week a different group makes the meals, and the lunches are sold as fundraisers for the church. Rodriguez has been coming to Cristo Rey for eight years. She completed all her catechism classes, was baptized and sings in one of Cristo Rey's choirs. Her decision to worship here is both personal and because of family. "In my personal opinion, we all come together—we're like a big family pretty much. We all get along no matter what the race is."

Across from the kitchen, around fifty people sit at a round table in La Virgen de Guadalupe Hall. They enjoy their gorditas, croissants and coffee in Styrofoam American Red Cross cups. Nino Rodriguez, a Spanish professor at Michigan State University, is teaching a Bible class to them. "Ven, dalo todo, sigueme," he says, discussing Christ's command to "come, give everything and follow me."

The diffused tungsten lights above him illuminate his thick, white hair. For about forty-five minutes he varies between rapid conviction-infused analogies, mandatos de Dios (commands from God) and compassionate commentaries.

A bell rings at 11:30, signaling the conclusion of the religious education program elsewhere in the church for about 200 children.

Noon Mass will soon begin.

TWO GIRLS IN white robes carry a tall wooden crucifix decorated with a fluttering, Kelly green ribbon. These altar servers help the priest during Mass. Their role is to light candles, carry the processional cross and set the altar for communion, among other duties.

"Welcome to the celebration of joy in the name del Padre, del Hijo y del Espíritu Santo." Father Thelen sings in Spanish with arms raised, displaying the enormous green sleeves of his robe. One of the altar servers raises a bookmarked prayer book for him to read from.

A large, stained-glass image of Jesus is the centerpiece of the sanctuary. Stylistically, it strongly reflects Our Lady of Guadalupe. Vibrant rays of the sun radiate from Jesus's bowed posture, and his face is depicted with Latino flair.

On the right side of the sanctuary, the presider's chair is beside the pews rather than on the platform to "emphasize the sense of community," says Father Thelen. On the left side stands a group of musicians leading worship. A woman and an elderly man wear brightly colored, striped wool shawls. Their garments' square shoulders and woven patterns shout authentic Latin culture, as do the musicians' rhythmic, minor-keyed songs. Instruments unfamiliar in most American church services await use, among them shakers, bongos and a washboard-like scraping instrument. The church has four choirs—one for each of its three services and a kids' choir. "Music speaks to people very strongly," Father Thelen notes.

The offering is collected in fabric cestas (baskets) a foot or so deep. A cheery, orange songbook titled *Flor y Canto* rests behind the uncushioned, wooden benches. Glass communion goblets with blue-lined rims wait at the front. Two girls wear all black with a rose pinned in each of their buns. Some worshippers clap. Children hug their parents' necks or crawl across the benches. Compared to Cristo Rey's bilingual service the same day, seemingly twice as many people attend the Spanish-language Mass.

CRISTO REY HISPANIC PARISH was founded in 1961 and for five years was located where Interstate 496 and Washington Avenue now cross until the parish was torn down to make room for the freeway.

Cristo Rey Community Center, which provides a medical clinic, counseling and other services, opened in 1968, and Mass was celebrated in the community center hall. The center and parish became separate institutions under separate leadership when the parish was re-established in 1979 on Washington Avenue. It moved to its current location in 1998.

Father Thelen has been a priest for thirty-three years but not only at Cristo Rey. After Spanish-language training in Bolivia, he lived in Peru for five years as a missionary among the Aymara Indians. He became the pastor of Cristo Rey in 1993.

Most congregants are Hispanic and from either Mexico or Texas. "I've kind of coined the term 'MichMex' or 'MichMexTex,'" Father Thelen chuckles. Some are from Puerto Rico, Colombia, Peru, Cuba and Mexico, among other places. Anglos also attend. "One misperception is that the church is only for Spanish-speaking people, when both Spanish and English are both equally celebrated here. English-speakers can feel comfortable." The church contains a strong cross-cultural atmosphere, especially when it holds Latin-Anglo weddings, he says.

The community center was placed under Father Thelen's leadership because of financial difficulties and now Cristo Rey Community Center is experiencing new energy and establishing more clearly defined goals under a new board of directors and new executive director.

Father Frederick Thelen says a closing prayer.

"**PEOPLE COMING FROM** the Latino cultures seem to have a very strong sense of faith, so their faith in God really integrates into everyday life," Father Thelen says. This focus on incorporating God into daily life is perhaps what inspired their commonly used phrase "Primero Dios" or "God first." Many parishioners are undocumented immigrants, Father Thelen points out, which might be one reason the church is so active in advocating for immigration reform. The church is involved in the Civil Rights for Immigrants Task Force, a task force of Action of Greater Lansing in which churches come together to advocate justice reform. Through the task force, Cristo Rey also addresses local concerns such as getting police departments to recognize Mexican IDs and drivers' licenses as valid proof of identity.

<hr />

MARTA ROMERO HAS attended Cristo Rey for years, as have her son, two daughters and many grandchildren. "We really enjoy it here because we can hear the sermon, the Mass, in Spanish. I can understand the Mass in English, but for some reason or another I prefer the Spanish." Now retired, Romero used to lead classes for baptism. She mourns young people's apathy toward faith and religious discipline. "Where is their faith? Young people don't take it seriously. When you live in the U.S., you are always busy."

In addition, Cristo Rey offers children's religious education programs, including first-grade catechism, pre-K through eighth grade Sunday school classes and youth group on Sunday evenings.

Guadalupe "Lupe" Castillo remembers when she started coming to Cristo Rey in 1988. "I felt at home, I felt at peace. And I thought 'I need to do something here,'" she says. Becoming coordinator of youth ministry was her solution. "It is most rewarding helping youth grow in their spiritual journey, being there for them as an advocate, and in not only their joys but their sadness."

Cristo Rey takes its youth to national conventions, including an annual convention held by the Diocese of Lansing and the National Catholic Youth Conference in Indianapolis attended by nearly 25,000 teenagers. "Not only within our parish do they experience our traditions," says Castillo, but the youth also experience "the bigger church, the body of Christ, outside."

Yet many people shy away from this ministry because youth are so complex, she says. "I'm not a counselor, by no means, but I have a good listening ear and so I think that's what they're looking for. They need someone they can trust, a shoulder to cry on."

Castillo says that being a Hispanic living in Michigan can be a drastic culture shock. She recalls leaving her home and how her school was "a whole different world. Our youth at Cristo Rey, they leave a Hispanic home in the morning and go to school, and they have to figure out how they're going to use their home lives and go to this other world. So they're leading two different lives."

Cristo Rey prides itself in its rich variety of religious and cultural celebrations. Many are listed on the back of the church bulletin. Among them are Posadas, Las Mañanitas, Dia de los Reyes, Dia de los Muertos, Candelaria and Virgen de la Divina Providencia. The church hosts popular fiestas with Latino music groups, food and dancing. Of particular importance is the Lady of Guadalupe feast day on December 12. A novena, nine days of prayer, leads up to the feast. The day before the feast, "La Virgin" serenata (serenade) for

The altar servers carry the processional cross.

Mary occurs, as well as prayers and reflections. The next morning at 6, mañanitas (early morning prayers) are dedicated to Our Lady of Guadalupe, with breakfast and feast day Mass following. Children often dress up in folkloric costumes, perform short plays and present roses to the image of Our Lady of Guadalupe—just as a devoted Juan Diego presented roses to the Bishop almost six centuries ago.

We're Trying to Build the Kingdom

— Discover Life Church, East Lansing

By Leah Benoit with photography by Ashley Weigel

PAINTED WHITE WITH tall pillars, the entrance to Discover Life in Lansing evokes a 1950s charm and innocence. Inside, bright pastels and shades of cream cast an aura reminiscent of sunlight and spring.

Pews are aligned along two central aisles where congregants walk back and forth to greet one another prior to the 11 a.m. service. With less than two minutes before the service is set to begin, most of the fifty or so worshippers—primarily white and middle-aged—make no effort to sit close to the front of the sanctuary, remaining spread throughout it.

People sit. A video begins to play on a projection screen. And hidden in plain view: Pastor Scott Hanson.

And that, he says, is the point. Dressed in casual khakis and a green sweater, Pastor Hanson blends in with the other worshippers. He doesn't lead the service. Instead, his wife Yvonne begins with a song. "Honestly, if somebody moves to Lansing and

Churchgoers socialize before the service.

they've been in a Baptist church in Tennessee for twenty years, they'd probably be a little uncomfortable," he says. "It's taken me some time to get over that."

Born in Alabama, Pastor Hanson spent his younger years attending what he refers to as a "traditional" Southern Baptist church. Initially planning to enlist in the military, he found himself drawn to the ministry after maturing spiritually in his late teens and early twenties. He became licensed as a minister with the approval of his home church before beginning a journey that took him from Alabama to New York, Metro Detroit and Pennsylvania before being called to Discover Life, then known as Bethany Baptist.

The organ music he was accustomed to as a child has been replaced with acoustic guitar and drums. There is no choir, and those who feel inspired to sing read the words from a slideshow presentation instead of books. Although Pastor Hanson previously preached at services of one hundred or more, Discover Life's Sunday worship attendance now fluctuates between fifty and seventy.

WHILE HIS APPROACH to worship could be viewed as a modernist approach to religion in today's world, the congregants believe it works for them. Their approach is all about being welcoming. "If someone wears jeans on Sunday morning, they won't stand out in a crowd," says Pastor Hanson. "I purposely don't wear ties so that somebody who walks in for the first time won't feel out of place.

"While I do want to be a vessel for God's message, it is my job to preach, but not my own experiences. I preach the truth from the Bible. I do share some of my own experiences but the Bible is the ultimate source of my preaching," he explains. It's a method also implemented through song. Referring to the church's lack of a formal choir, he sees the opportunity for all worshippers, not just those with vocal ability, to sing as a way that unites congregants and keeps them on the same level.

And so they sing:

> *How great is our God—sing with me*
> *How great is our God—and all will see*
> *How great, how great is our God.*

As the projection screen displays the words, members follow along. The songs feature predominantly major chord progressions, giving them a bright and optimistic tone that differs greatly from much traditional religious organ music. There is no music to read, unlike in traditional hymnals, and the worship team practices hard. As the pastor explains, "Our goal is to connect. If you only have the best singers, or only preach about success rather than failure, you put your members at a different level. We need to be united."

Unity remains a theme throughout the service. While Yvonne Hanson begins the service, another member concludes it with a prayer. Pastor Hanson sits with his family in the pews, rather than taking a place at the head of the chapel, until the music portion of the service finishes. Congregants hold hands, embrace and shout agreement. He then gets up to preach. The message this day is mercy.

MEMBERSHIP ISN'T WHAT it once was for Discover Life. It has two buildings on the property, one that houses the church and small classrooms and another that hosts Bible study activities and classes. There are rooms for children of varying ages, complete with toys and books. Yet the rooms are used, at most, three times a week. In addition, a Hispanic Baptist church group uses Discover Life while it raises money for a space of its own.

Although he considers his faith to be his true profession, Pastor Hanson works full-

Hymnals in the pews
of the sanctuary

time at an insurance company during the week. The situation is not ideal, but he says the church has been extraordinarily supportive. "If someone has surgery at 10 in the morning, I can't be there. Whereas before, nobody went in for surgery without me being there to pray with them and talk with them and their families."

While he hopes Discover Life will continue to increase its membership, he stresses that his measure of success has nothing to do with numbers. It's about something more.

"Guys that go into a church and it doubles or triples membership in a year are asked to write books—no one is asking me to write a book. We've gone from approximately thirty to seventy in seven years. But my wife and I see the progress that people are making and are getting more folks involved. I'm not worried about numbers. Numbers will take care of themselves."

THE CHURCH HAS adopted a low-income neighborhood in Lansing as part of its community outreach. Annually, members knock on doors and deliver homemade cookies around the Christmas holiday season. They've donated Bibles, batteries for smoke detectors and other items in hopes of spreading God's love. A back-to-school event saw thirty members help more than 150 community residents by giving away backpacks, cotton candy and school supplies.

Here, Pastor Hanson finds his biggest source of joy, "joy at watching those in the church growing in their faith and reaching outside their comfort zone to help others." While it's easier to go to less impoverished neighborhoods, the response from those they help is overwhelming. It wasn't easy for congregants to warm up to the idea initially, with some expressing fear of even entering the neighborhood, he notes, but they understand the importance of continuing to give to the community. "From the beginning, we were told if we were going to show up once and never come back to not even bother. The kids and families need something positive and consistent, and we can help." While they also hope the congregation grows, they go into the neighborhoods "to tell them about Jesus and His love and hope to one day disciple or teach them what it means to live for God."

In addition to outreach, having new members identify with Discover Life's message is essential. Misconceptions about his faith don't faze Pastor Hanson, nor are they ignored. He notes that in popular culture, Baptists—particularly those of the Southern Baptist denominations—tend to have a reputation of being a bit extreme. The church's name change, from Bethany Baptist to Discover Life, was intended to draw potential members looking for a new faith or trying to establish one for the first time. The church believed that cutting "Bethany Baptist" from the name would sound more inviting.

And inviting they are. Non-members who observe a service quickly feel welcome and are greeted personally by nearly every individual in attendance. Visitors don't always return, but Pastor Hanson isn't worried. The goal, he says, is to lead them to Christ, not necessarily to Discover Life in particular. "If somebody already has a church, we aren't trying to pull them out of that. If we visit somebody and they haven't been to church in a while, and they go to church with their mom the next day, we win," he says. "We're not just focusing on our church—we're trying to build the Kingdom."

Sharing Our Blessings
— Eastminster Presbyterian Church, East Lansing

By Duygu Kanver with photography by Brittany Holmes

There is a big, white Celtic cross on the west side of Abbot Road. Many people in the many cars heading toward downtown East Lansing pass by it every day. Students driving from their apartment complexes to Michigan State University's campus and young adults on their way home after dropping off a package at the post office pass the big, white Celtic cross. How many are aware that this church, Eastminster Presbyterian Church, is on their familiar route?

But this church is there, hidden in a vast yard covered with grass and trees, away from the busy road, yet very much in the city center. Reverend Margie Osborn says the big, white cross by the road was erected a year before she was called to be the church's pastor in 2005: "Before that, our church would go completely unnoticed."

Of course, it's only the building that goes unnoticed. Eastminster is a large congregation of approximately 210 adult

Donations are essential to the operation of the church.

members and fifty children. About one-third of the members attend the Sunday service this morning. There are eight rows of long pews on two sides of the pentagon-shaped sanctuary. No row is empty. Worshippers are seated all around the sanctuary, and the middle rows are densely occupied.

Behind the pulpit at the top corner of the pentagon is a carved window screen. Rays of sun in different shapes gleam over a table on the pulpit with its open Bible flanked by two candles. It is a bright room, thanks to the natural light coming in through twenty-four tall windows—six each on four sides of the pentagon. Through the windows is a view of trees and fallen leaves, and it's impossible to see Abbot Road. The view through the church windows makes members feel closer to God and his creation. Reverend Osborn thinks everyone and everything are blessed with some good feature, and one such blessing is this churchyard.

Behind the pews, close to the entrance of the sanctuary, is a wooden organ, the second-best in the area, Reverend Osborn claims. Edisher Savitski, who earned his Doctor of Musical Arts degree from Michigan State, plays the prelude, Adagio, which marks the beginning of the Sunday service. Along with Savitski's playing, the hymns of the adult choir prepare the congregants for the service as well. One cannot help but notice the facial expressions of the choir director Stuart Hill. A first-year doctoral student in music education, Hill is a passionate musician and devoted Christian who was raised Presbyterian. With these two qualities combined, his deep commitment to his job becomes visible, and everyone can see how immersed he is in his music as he waves his arms and swings his baton.

Music plays a big role in many places of worship, but at Eastminster Presbyterian, one can feel the power of music strongly. The first line of the call to worship reads, "It is good to praise the Lord and make music to your name, O Most High," an appropriate line that emphasizes the meaning of music in this house of God.

ONE CAN UNDERSTAND what is particularly important to the Eastminster Presbyterian community just by being in the sanctuary for this Sunday service. As with the power of music, the importance of children is felt as the service continues. A children's message time is nothing unusual—a lot of churches include one in their worship programs—but here it feels somehow different, somehow more special.

After the kids are called forward, a congregant steps up with a grocery bag in her hand. Her name is Beverly Bonning and, although she is an attorney, she has spent a lot of time on children's education and has taught in the Sunday school for fifteen years. She sits with the kids and starts to take out bright red Michigan apples from the bag, introducing a few of the many varieties grown in the state. Gala, Jonathan and Honeycrisp appear one by one. Then she shows different products made with apples: a pie, a jar of applesauce, a bottle of cider. "See," she explains, "there are many types of apples and each of them is good for different purposes. Human beings are like that, too." In a simple yet captivating talk, Bonning teaches the children a valuable lesson: that everyone is gifted with different qualities and that they should use them to do good deeds in life. "Bev is just remarkable," says Reverend Osborn.

She's not the only member who is good with the kids. Every Sunday, another volunteer prepares the children's message time. After Bonning's message, 8-year-old Alida Wyble's birthday is celebrated while she's in the front, and the congregants sing "Happy Birthday."

Alida and her older brother Fletcher have been active participants in other

Reverend Margie Osborn works to make each congregant feel like part of the church family.

events in Eastminster too. Reverend Osborn tells how Alida said, "I'm so excited, and I'm so nervous!" as she and her brother were about to call the worship and the prayer of confession while serving as liturgists a few weeks earlier. Two weeks after Easter, on Youth Sunday, 12-year-old Fletcher delivered a sermon he had written himself and, according to Reverend Osborn, did a superb job. "It had humor, personal illustrations. It was good and everyone was impressed."

Reverend Osborn is also happy that most congregants attend Youth Sundays, and she's proud to lead a community that highly values children and includes them as much as possible. "They are not an add-on—they are a part of the community, and we need them. We try to find meaningful things for them to do; ways that they can enrich us as adults." Alida and Fletcher's participation is just one example of the roles children play in the church—a young girl plays the offertory on the piano, and children bring the bread and the wine for the Communion service once every month.

TODAY'S SERMON IS very much about children as well. As Reverend Osborn tells the miraculous story from the Gospels of Matthew, Mark and Luke of a boy who provided food for Jesus's horde, she advises congregants not to dismiss children and their ideas. In a conversation after the service, she explains how great it feels to see them grow up before

Reverend Margie Osborn reads a passage from the Bible explaining the importance of giving.

her eyes, and she mentions how delightful it is to see the ones who go off to college come back at Christmastime. She hasn't been at Eastminster Presbyterian long enough to see any of them get married, but officiating at such a wedding is her dream.

Children, young adults and senior congregants are all part of the church, a nice mix of people of different ages, but not all ages are well-represented. Like most other worship places in the area, undergraduates don't often attend services. She's glad when an under-graduate from Michigan State visits, but she doesn't protest when students can't or don't come to church. She understands that college students are usually busy with classes, extra-curricular activities, internships and job searches. Rather than trying to change people's minds or make them attend, Reverend Osborn and members of the church develop plans that will enable them to share their faith in Jesus and invite anyone who wants to come find out more about their faith.

THE NINE-ACRE PROPERTY the church owns is a blessing that makes the church unique among others in the area, Reverend Osborn says. Like Bonning talking with the children as part of the service, this land is a gift of Eastminster Presbyterian, and members should find ways to use it for good purposes, she says. She is working with a team to implement a landscape design that will welcome everyone in the area. In its vast yard will be a labyrinth for meditation, a prayer path in the woods and a rain garden for wildflowers and butterflies. All will be open to the public.

"We are hoping to develop an outdoor space that will be inviting to the community," she says, "but no strings attached. All we want is to share our blessings with the community. Of course, if visitors want to know about us and decide to attend the church, it will be great."

The plans include handicapped accessibility so that people can come with wheelchairs, walkers and baby strollers. When the gardens are complete, the church wants to organize big cookouts a couple of times a year for the community, especially Michigan State students. "Our neighbors in the community are already coming to play baseball on our field, to ride their skateboards up in the driveway and to walk their dogs on our property. We'd like them to know that it's okay—that they are not trespassing but rather are welcome here."

Exciting plans are taking place in this hard-to-spot churchyard on Abbot Road. Members or not, there will soon be many people enjoying themselves in the yard behind the big, white Celtic cross. More people will become familiar with Eastminster Presbyterian, and it will be able to share its blessings with more people.

Congregants share their faith through singing together.

8

A Duty to Save Souls

— Episcopal Church of St. Michael the Archangel, East Lansing

By Marisa Hamel with photography by Erin Hampton

T HE WOOD-FRAMED GLASS doors of the Episcopal Church of St. Michael seem to hold up the shell of the tall, hollow building filled with warm air and the echoing of an organ on a Sunday morning before Eucharist.

Anglican history and Roman Catholic tradition meld into the creeds and sacraments held holy by this ministry. Episcopalians call themselves "ancient and reformed" and "liberal and conservative," with clergy taking the same vows of obedience as Catholic priests, but opening the religious life to ordained women as leaders of the priests and deacons in the diocese. The Episcopal Church, by doctrine and democratic process of amending canon law, is accepting of those who may feel marginalized or outside the norm; LGBT groups are active in many parishes, for example, and even pets can be brought to and blessed at the services. Hugs during worship and swapping banana bread recipes at coffee hour are a staple at St. Michael's.

Father Roger Walker reads from the *Book of Common Prayer* as the congregation follows along.

Father Roger Walker might jokingly support the idea that "ancient" is an appropriate word for his congregation. "Let me put that into perspective," he says with a mellow Southern accent, because "we can't brag about that" if the church seeks to attract young people and children. St. Michael's was built in the 1950s, a time of economic vitality after World War II when homes and churches sprang up in the area. St. Michael's was established as a "storefront" mission church to serve South Lansing, and church records show that the pews were tightly packed with tightly packed with as many as 200 parishioners on Sundays. "It was a boom time. This church was built in that boom period."

Over the next few decades, the economy settled into equilibrium. Then families moved away from the church and the community for any number of reasons: jobs, college, lack of faith. Children grew up. Parents aged. And, as Father Walker observes, "Demographics change in the neighborhood and congregations change. This has been church history—it waxes and wanes." From a historical perspective, that's not unusual and could even be anticipated, but now St. Michael's continues with some of its original members.

Now, he says St. Michael's pulls around fifty worshippers to its two Sunday services, most of them older than 50. Even so, he notes, the church doesn't lack diversity. A lesbian couple, a parishioner from Africa and a woman with a seeing-eye dog are in attendance on any given week. He jokes, "We even have straight people here."

There is an upside to a small congregation: talking before the service, hugging each other on their way in and making sure visitors are invited back five times before they exit the dimly sparkling stained glass doors.

As with any group, there are disagreements, which Father Walker considers a healthy trait of his parishioners. Positive, healthy disagreement sparks change and creativity, and he believes St. Michael's is more democratic for fostering such respectful debates and divergent opinions within Episcopal traditions. "If I had people here that always agreed with one another, I'd really be worried about them. The people I get concerned about are the ones who brood."

Patience and confrontation are also qualities of Episcopalians, it seems. Father Walker has confronted a few "parking lot church" meetings, where parishioners talk about the problems of the church in the absence of the people who might actually help fix them.

Father Walker is from Louisville, Kentucky. He was ordained at age 51 and calls himself a "late bloomer." His first career was in social work, so he brings experience building interpersonal relationships to his church community. What sets his parish apart, he says, is its welcoming atmosphere intertwined with the holy traditions of the Eucharist. He's been at St. Michael's for only a year.

"THE SERVICE HERE is more laid-back than the big uptown church," Father Walker says. The organist plays "Happy Birthday" for a parishioner as congregants shuffle in for the 10:30 a.m. service. The congregants settle into their sparse spots in the pews and hum a familiar hymn during the processional as Father Walker and Guest Preacher Father Andrew Shirota of All Saints Episcopal Church in East Lansing walk to the altar. Their cinctured white albs and wooden crosses sway in unison in front of the congregation. Praise, confession and solemn peace blessings follow. Baptized worshippers file across the altar and kneel in a semi-circle, hands extended to receive communion.

Father Shirota's sermon reminds the congregation to be thankful, reflective and prayerful in their lives. Many come to seek God in times of hardship, he tells them, but the focus of a relationship with God should be to give as well as take—giving time, prayer and faith to God in addition to receiving His grace. The New Testament lesson in Timothy 2:8 read during the service reassures the faithful of God's unconditional love, despite human sin:

> If we have died with Him, we will also live with Him;
> If we endure, we will also reign with Him
> If we deny Him, He will also deny us;
> If we are faithless, He remains faithful—
> For He cannot deny Himself.

As the sermon closes, Father Shirota asks the congregants why they return every Sunday. Why go to St. Michael's and not to another church? He answers his own questions: it's a question of faith and a personal calling. He compares it with the Apostle Paul's faith

Lay Minister Judith Ramsey exchanges the Peace with congregants during the service.

that Jesus was his rock who called him to spread the Gospel and write letters to those Jesus could not reach.

For Father Walker, the sacred text and prayers of the people bring worship alive. There is a distinct human and holy element to leading a worship service that a priest can bring the Eucharist, Christ Himself, to those he loves and lives to serve. Being on the altar is more than giving blessings and officiating at weddings and more often nowadays, funerals. A priest's key responsibility is a duty to save souls, a heavy and serious mission to be accomplished in kindness and love. "I feel a great deal of responsibility for them as parishioners and for their souls," he explains. "Part of what a priest does is accept the responsibility of leading others to and building the relationship with God, so sometimes I have to admit, I back up and say, 'Who am I to be doing this? I'm having my own struggles.'"

Aside from the gravity of his position, Father Walker is admittedly human. To illustrate, he recalls one service where a woman smartly "talked back" during the peace offering to counter one of the points in his sermon. He accepts criticism, not aiming to be above his parishioners but to serve them. He is, after all, exactly like them. "There's not a Sunday goes by that I don't screw up on something," he laughs.

***

St. Michael's is a church in need. Many members are elderly and dealing with illness or financial problems. Much of Father Walker's time is spent in pastoral ministry, serving the ill, the homebound and those "suffering crises in their life, in their loves, in their health."

Father Roger Walker and Lay Minister Barry Baker take Communion.

These are the tender, private parts of their lives that church members share with him. "People come forward and hold out their hands for the Host, and you know what's going on in their lives when they receive it. It's touching to see them there and to know."

Father Walker's mother is sick with pancreatic cancer, which takes him away from ministry but helps him understand similar struggles in others' lives. Despite disagreements among church members, prayers and notes of support flow to him, and he knows they truly have others' interests at heart.

This is an established church, a home where grandmothers and retirees have been coming since their children were born, grew up and moved away. For them, it is their last stronghold of the past and has now become their family, a church family. They know when times get rough, as they do in old age, they will have this family to turn to.

"The church has potential, but potential will not get things done," says Father Walker. "Now we're in another period of transition. The congregation here, to be honest, is at a point where it will have to decide: So do we have a reason to continue to exist in this spot?" The church is tired, he admits. Members who sustained it for decades are at retirement age and even now, the number of volunteers for the Altar Guild is dwindling. Parishioners have left for retirement communities, and, frankly he says, many have died.

"For any congregation to survive, they have to feel they have a mission and a reason to exist," he says. A handful of members are gathering a workgroup to reevaluate the priorities of St. Michael's and those of a modern church. The challenge of maintaining the building itself is crippling on a meager budget for maintenance and upkeep. Several small Episcopal parishes in the area may be willing to share resources such as budgets, staffs and ministries so valuable services continue to extend across communities.

While St. Michael's welcomes newcomers, it isn't recruiting door-to-door for new members. But as Father Walker drives through the streets past Laundromats and diners, he hopes to find interest and brick-and-mortar grants with the congregation's support. The need for the ministry is here in the church's socioeconomically disadvantaged neighborhood, but word-of-mouth invitations are what draw people to worship. "You can have all the barbecues you want, but that's only an opportunity to invite people to the service."

Instead of weary disappointment at the thought of St. Michael's closing, Father Walker sees a possible positive future:

> A church has a life, a business has a life, as long as there's a mission for it to live. But there may come a day when this congregation says, 'It's time. We've done what we can, we've been here for fifty-some years and during that time we've done a good job, so we can close the doors and go to another church.' But some day some other church, some Baptist church, may come along and say, 'Hey, that's a nice building,' and start all over again with a whole new theology and approach to a whole new demographic. There's nothing wrong with that.

Julia Walton plays the organ at the Episcopal Church of St. Michael the Archangel.

Turn to God Alone

— First Church of Christ, Scientist of Greater
Lansing, East Lansing

By Joshua Anderson with photography by Katie Stiefel

THOSE USED TO most typical Christian churches may be surprised to find that the First Church of Christ, Scientist is a lay institution without clergy. Two members stand before the congregation to conduct the Sunday service by reading from the Bible and *Science and Health with Key to the Scriptures* by Mary Baker Eddy, the two books they use as their Pastor.

An antique copy of *Science and Health* is encased in Plexiglas in the church's anteroom, waiting to catch the attention of a long-time member or curious newcomer. A delicate white glove rests beside the massive volume to protect it from damage.

That isn't to say that seekers are discouraged from perusing the book's cream-colored pages. Eddy's manuscript, published in 1875, is an essential tool of disseminating the church's stated goal of commemorating "the word and works of our Master, which should reinstate primitive Christianity and its lost element of healing." Other copies of the book can be found throughout the

Russell Wright and Carol Rounds read to the congregation.

church and in the Reading Room.

That "Master" is Jesus Christ, and the podium inside the church bears two quotations—one from the Bible and one from *Science and Health*. On Sunday, two readers stand before the congregation, one reading from the Bible and the other reading passages from *Science and Health*. Both books are vital to believers' growth in Christian Science.

The church has shelves of biographies about Eddy for sale in its Reading Room for students from Michigan State University across the street and to other visitors who stop by. There's simply no way to talk about Christian Science without mentioning its Founder or, as members say, its "discoverer."

As a faith, Christ and Christianity are central to Christian Science. And as its Founder, Eddy is essential to the church. It's a church that avoids placing authority in earthly figures. During services, "there's no personality up there dictating what the Bible means to them and what it should mean to us," says Deborah Wright, head usher and a board member of the church. "We get it directly from God and from the Bible."

THIS EMPHASIS ON individual spiritual growth is personified by the church's signature Reading Room, a round structure protruding from the front of the building. It's not a lecture room with space for a speaker to "read" lessons aloud to a congregation. No, all the reading is done on one's own.

The Reading Room's distinctive architecture is eye-catching to those passing the corner of East Grand River Avenue and Collingwood Road. Inside, visitors can grab a volume of Christian Science-related reading material, sink into a plump chair and, on colder nights, keep warm in front of a fireplace. The panoramic windows of the Reading Room offer a view of the edge of the campus, often bustling with students eyeing the curved outer walls of the building.

The Christian Science headquarters in Boston, Massachusetts—referred to by members as the "Mother Church"—publishes a substantial amount of material that finds its way to Reading Rooms across the world. Its best-known publication is *The Christian Science Monitor*, a Pulitzer Prize-winning newspaper that reports on everything from world news to business, science, pop culture and more. Eddy started the *Monitor* in 1908 as a response to the yellow journalism of the time. Her perspective is evidenced by the newspaper's slogan: "To injure no man, but to bless all mankind." The name of the newspaper is derived from Eddy's policy of honesty and transparency. She knew that taking the words "Christian Science" out of the title might allow it to reach a wider audience, but she didn't want to mislead anyone about the organization behind the *Monitor*. The paper publishes one article every day from "a Christian Science perspective," just as Eddy requested back at its 1908 founding.

The reading material doesn't stop there. Weekly issues of the magazine *The Christian Science Sentinel* are filled with testimonies of Christian Scientists experiencing God's healing. Another publication, *The Christian Science Quarterly*, compiles Bible lessons on which the coming months' Sunday services are based. It lists passages from the faith's two central texts so members can read and meditate on their themes ahead of time. For advanced readers, *The Christian Science Journal* contains in-depth articles about healings and a directory of Christian Science nurses and practitioners, people whom the church believes have demonstrated a history of being able to heal using Christian Science.

THE RELIGION IS known for its emphasis on healing, encouraging its members to turn to God alone when confronted with an illness. That said, the church does not shun members for visiting health clinics or using conventional medicine, leaving such decisions to the individual based on his or her own level of faith.

Every Wednesday night, the East Lansing church provides an opportunity for members to share the ways God has worked in their lives. After readings and hymns, an usher grabs a microphone and offers it to anyone who feels inspired to speak. At first, there's an awkward silence as members look down at their shoes, perhaps mustering the courage to speak or quietly nudging the person next to them to do so. Finally, someone volunteers with a raised hand, and the usher's face lights up.

Taking the microphone, Jeanne Troutman describes a healing she experienced the previous week—she fell from her porch and hurt her ankle. Whether it was broken or sprained isn't specified, because she never asked for a doctor's diagnosis. Fighting through the pain, she went back inside her home, laid in bed and prayed for help. By the time she was able to come to the Wednesday service and tell her story, the pain was all gone.

Wright, the head usher, shares the story of her brush with death as a child. Wandering away from her parents, she drank turpentine—that's what she's been told happened, as she has no recollection of the event. When her parents found her, her skin had turned blue and she wasn't breathing. Her parents called an ambulance, but, while waiting for it to arrive, Wright says her father felt an angel and remembered God's love. When she finally made it to the hospital, it appeared as if the harsh effects of the chemical were disappearing. All the doctors prescribed was a bland diet, and with that, she recovered.

Not every story shared at Wednesday night services is about a miraculous healing. Often, a congregant simply wants to express gratitude to God for His help through a trying situation. One woman attributes to God her ability to forgive a relative for a past wrongdoing. Carol Rounds, a longtime member and one of the two Sunday readers, describes how God recently helped assuage her feelings of impatience while she was stuck in traffic.

Rounds describes the outlook that Christian Science has given her about humankind: "We know no more about man that we know about God." Since man is made in God's image, to see what man is like, one must first see what God is like, she says.

This benevolent view allows members to look past their neighbors' faults and see the good inside them. As a result, many spend their free time helping others at a soup kitchen, in the Peace Corps, at a food pantry and elsewhere. While the church itself doesn't host many such activities, its members often seek them on their own. "It's not a necessary part of our religion," says Rounds. "It just seems to happen." Wright elaborates on the role of the church in planting the seeds of community service: "We're educated through reading the lesson or Bible study, and then we can go out individually through the community and make a difference."

In keeping with the general simplicity of its services, worship has a soloist rather than a choir. "We believe that church is for individual spiritual growth. We don't want to take up

A copy of *Science and Health with Key to the Scriptures* written by Mary Baker Eddy

people's time," explains Rounds. She loves to sing hymns, but she insists that if she wanted to join a choir, she'd join one in the community. As she puts it, "Church is your time to learn more about God and devote your thought to your relationship with God, and choir time often turns into busy time."

Since faith is personal, Christian Science views its role not as an instigator but as an encourager. The church doesn't push anyone too hard to adopt its teachings, but instead offers a wealth of resources so individuals can reach conclusions on their own.

Members often speak of gratefulness: gratefulness to God, gratefulness for the healing power of Christian Science, gratefulness to each other. No matter what country a church is in, there's always a yearly Thanksgiving service. Like the American Pilgrims of yore, Christian Scientists give thanks for their blessings, achieved in part by their own hard work in studying and applying their faith but also received from God on high. There's room to

Member Jeanne Troutman holds a book of hymns during a Thursday night service.

be proud of one's accomplishments through Christian Science. Rounds, for example, says she's the happiest she's ever been because of her years of living by the principles of the faith. Even so, services, especially those on Wednesday nights, are characterized by a feeling of gratitude toward those who've helped the congregants along their way.

Meg Vogler, a member who gives back to her church by producing Braille versions of Christian Science reading material, stands in the anteroom of the sanctuary one Wednesday night after the service. She's surrounded by congregants she's known for years, all of them talking to one another like friends. With a smile and a bright voice, Vogler sums up the mood of the night, and thus, of the church itself: "It's like Thanksgiving every week."

First Church of Christ, Scientist

10

Right Worship
— Holy Trinity Greek Orthodox Church, Lansing

By Yvonne Makidon, Ph.D., with photography by Andrea Raby

A TALL WHITE spire gleams in the morning sun as the parking lot begins filling up. It is ten minutes before the start of the service. Across the street sits a large modern building—Lansing Catholic Central High School. Holy Trinity sits between a four-lane boulevard with one-way traffic running up both sides, which links to Route 127. This area has an industrial and businesslike feel to it—there are no homes, and it is surreal to leave the business-industrial vibe to enter a more spiritual world.

Upon entry into Holy Trinity Greek Orthodox Church, one feels a shift in the ambience. An Old-World feel permeates the atmosphere and transports visitors and worshippers from the present into the past. A male voice chants and sings in Greek and English, haunting and inviting.

The view into the sanctuary through the glass windows in the narthex (antechamber) is breathtaking, a feast for the eyes.

Iconography and stained glass windows usher worshippers into God's presence. The altar sits behind a series of icons—paintings topped with elaborate scrollwork arches that define the space between altar and pews. The screen represents a "cloud of witnesses" calling human beings into the unseen realm of God. Behind the screens, a mystery unfolds. Altar boys assist the priest in performing worship rituals as necks strain to watch them. Awe and wonderment unfold. Incense pumps into the air from the censer held by the priest while congregants continue to enter for the service. The eyes are drawn forward and upward. The ears follow the voices of the yet-unseen choir. The nose is drawn into the experience, and a heightened sense of curiosity expands in the soul.

Everything is done with a purpose. Orchestrated from age-old traditions, the right worship is felt, seen, smelled and heard from the moment one enters. The outside world is forgotten. This place is removed—everything that is not worthy is left at the door. A cantor stands to the right of the altar, almost hidden below the icons and wooden beams. He and Father Mark Sietsema exchange chants and songs as offerings to God. They speak in code as if asking God for permission to worship.

A blue-robed choir sits above on a balcony, and their voices intermingle with those of the priest and the cantor. Almost everything is sung in this church, both in Greek and in English. Father Mark believes that "singing is the most natural expression of praise there is." Some parishioners accompany the choir, but many sit in silent reverence.

The sanctuary is designed to inspire awe. Worship can be done by just sitting and absorbing. One cannot help but be inspired to think of God in this place: Does He notice me? Am I acceptable?

Father Mark, who has been Holy Trinity's priest for thirteen years, defines Orthodoxy as "right worship." The Greek Orthodox Church focuses on "the worship—we focus on God." After the service, Father Mark's wife explains how the church engages all five senses during Sunday morning worship. The eyes observe the icons. The ears hear the singing. The mouth tastes the bread and wine. The nose inhales the smell of the incense. Congregants making the sign of the cross on their chests involve the sense of touch. All are purposefully done to invite people into God's presence.

Father Mark exudes pride as he narrates the background of the iconography at Holy Trinity. Icons by Cretan-born artist George Filippakis are fairly recent additions to this sanctuary, and their acquisition is considered one of the higher achievements for this parish. The icons depict religious scenes involving Jesus, the disciples and saints. The purpose of icons is to remind congregants of the rich traditions of the Greek Orthodox Church and to tell the story and the dogmas of who the saints and disciples were and what they believed. Father Mark describes the impact of iconography on believers:

"The icons remind us we are a small part of a much larger whole. We join the saints

A boy lights a candle at the beginning of the service. Candles are lit as prayers for loved ones both living and dead.

in that journey to the kingdom. We are a link in a chain. We are not alone, but we are surrounded by faces. Spiritual life as a solo journey just doesn't work."

When asked about the altar and the space behind the screens, he says it signifies the "Kingdom of God. We are all pressing to go behind the enclosure."

THERE ARE 150 people present during the service, some of them women wearing scarves on their heads. Congregants are both participants and observers to everything going on around them, partakers and witnesses to a sacred event. Chanting and singing fill the background as the priest and the altar boys carry a large Bible ensconced in a gold case from behind the enclosure. Ceremony is important: the priest wears rich white robes, and the altar boys are similarly dressed. It seems everything is elegantly designed to evoke awe and wonder—the right worship of God.

After the reading of the Gospel, an elaborate Communion takes place. The priest and altar boys perform a processional of the body and blood of Christ around the sanctuary. All the while, the priest sings and the congregation turns and faces the Sacrament as it passes by. After the processional, congregants of all ages line up in the middle aisle to receive a spoonful of the Sacrament from Father Mark, who communes each person by name. When stepping to the side, each congregant takes a small cube of bread.

This Sunday represents a rare opportunity for visitors: a 40-day-old baby girl is being presented to the church in a ritual referred to as the 40-Day Blessing. The tradition traces back to the days when Jesus's parents presented him at the Jewish Temple in the Holy Land. Congregants stand as Father Mark meets the family at the entrance to the sanctuary. He reaches out for the baby girl. Mother and father look on nervously as he holds the child, chants a prayer and performs the blessing. The act is both intimate and full of grandeur. As the family watches and follows him, he brings the child to the front of the screened enclosure at the altar and, through lifting motions, presents her to God. Once again, this blessing is designed to inspire, designed to draw in the worshipper.

After the blessing, it becomes apparent that the end of the service nears. A sense of joy emanates from the sanctuary. Congregants are invited to sit for a series of announcements. They are also invited to take more cubes of bread as they exit the sanctuary. The cube is a small reminder of the past one and a half hours as they return to their vehicles and the business of the day.

"NOT ALL MEMBERS of the congregation are ethnically Greek," says Father Mark. Among the other ethnicities belonging to Holy Trinity are Lebanese, Romanian, Serbian, Ethiopian

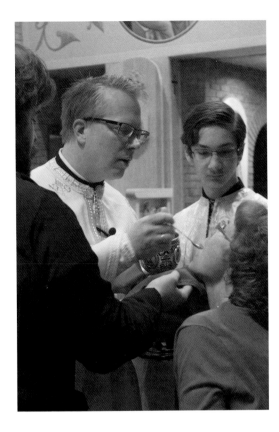

Father Mark Sietsema
feeds a woman wine
during Communion.

and Coptic. A mix of white-collar workers and business owners worship together with Michigan State University professors and graduate students.

Father Mark explains that the Orthodox Church is a confederation of thirteen sister churches around the world. There is no centralized body, and each has its own primate. Holy Trinity's patriarch is in Istanbul, Turkey.

The priest plays a paternal role here: supporter, provider, nurturer, counselor and caretaker of the congregants' spiritual and financial needs. And he, in turn, expects his parishioners to "try to be Christian." This church preserves an "ancient form of worship which has stood the test of time through many cultures," and Father Mark says people find spiritual strength through the Orthodox Church. Their focus is worship, a central tenet of their faith.

There are misconceptions in the community about the Greek Orthodox Church, he says. "We are not standoffish, and we don't mean to be. We are not always invited to other

Iconography on the ceiling of the sanctuary

religious events in the area." He's unsure why some other churches see the Greek Orthodox Church as different or outside of the circle of world Christianity.

He describes an event a few years ago when a Florida pastor wanted to come to Lansing to burn a Qur'an. The mayor worked to unite the faith communities to stop the Southern pastor, and Holy Trinity hosted the event. Father Mark does not recall getting a lot of press attention for Holy Trinity's role but later found out that "Muslims in the area remembered our participation. We spoke out on their behalf and they were grateful." He sees this as evidence of the church's subtle influence in the community.

Asked about future challenges, he responds:

> Greek Orthodox parishes had a strong sense of community fed by common ethnic ties. Today people have busier lives, sports at school, practices, and parents are busier now. This puts stress on this church's sense of community. This was the social center of the family. Now the social life of younger families is drawn away from the church. There isn't time in a family's week for the events that once filled the church calendar.

The Greek Orthodox Church faces challenges to staying current and connected, he continues, as its members "stand on the shoulders of those before who were connected to Jesus and the Apostles. They worship the living God in a traditional and ancient way that represents who they are in the community."

The congregation rises as Father Mark Sietsema reads a prayer in front of the altar. Altar boys hold the processional candles.

Father Mark Sietsema presents the bread and wine before Communion. Altar boys hold the exapteryga (icons of seraphim) and the processional cross.

Father Mark Sietsema delivers the 40-Day Blessing to a new member of the congregation.

11

Hasten to Prayer
— Islamic Center of East Lansing

By Tyler Hendon with photography by Dylan Sowle

A s you enter the Islamic Center of East Lansing, you see
the "ninety-nine names of God" on the mosque wall on
the left-hand side. Some of the names include "The All-Seeing,"
"The Grateful" and "The Ever-Providing." A large photo of Mecca
covers the right wall.

Michigan State University students with a drive to create
a home for praise and worship built the mosque in 1979. Since
then, the mosque has seen a diverse group of leaders who have
contributed to the Islamic Center's overall success.

The mosque holds five services a day. The adhan (the call to
prayer) hums over the loudspeaker as the service begins:

God is great, God is great,
God is great, God is great,
I bear witness that there is no god but God,
I bear witness that there is no god but God,
I bear witness that Muhammad is the messenger of God,

A Qur'an in the Islamic Center's library

I bear witness that Muhammad is the messenger of God,
Hasten to prayer, hasten to prayer,
Hasten to success, hasten to success,
God is great, God is great,
There is no God but God.

As the adhan ends, Muslims of many ethnicities and ages pour into the sanctuary, but some don't arrive until the service is well underway.

Professor Mohammad Khalil, director of the Muslim Studies Program at Michigan State, explains that Islam means submission to God, but here "submission" has a positive connotation "because God represents all things good."

He informs visitors that speaking is frowned upon during the service. "Nonetheless, not everyone follows the rules, which is why a small minority might still whisper during the service." Shoes aren't allowed within the sanctuary, so worshippers leave their shoes on racks along the wall. Worshippers sit close to each other, praying quietly and waiting for

Members greet each other after an early service. Their style of dress varies from traditional to modern.

the imam to enter. A father motions for his sons to sit as they walk in late. He frantically waves his hands to get their attention. The boys are very young, but they still understand the importance of silence.

The sanctuary is full, so some men pray outside it. A few stand side-by-side, close to the entrance of the sanctuary.

The imam, Mohamed Mabrouk, begins by saying, "We seek refuge in Allah from the evil within ourselves and the evil within our sins. I urge you to practice patience in the little aspects of life."

KHALIL RECEIVED HIS bachelor's, master's and doctorate degrees from the University of Michigan. He serves as an associate professor of religious studies at Michigan State and previously served as an assistant professor of religion and visiting professor of law at the University of Illinois. He's also been a devoted member of the Islamic Center of East Lansing since his childhood.

He takes time to explain the Five Pillars of Islam to a few guests at the mosque. The first pillar is "to declare your faith, accepting that there is one God and accepting that Muhammad was a messenger of God." Muslims also see Abraham, Moses and Jesus as messengers. Jesus plays an important role in the Qur'an, and while not considered divine, he is regarded as a special prophet. The second pillar of faith is prayer. Muslims are expected to pray five times a day, and each prayer typically lasts five minutes. He continues:

The main prayer room often reaches capacity, so some worshippers pray outside its doors.

The third is to give to the poor. The fourth is fasting in the month of Ramadan, when one refrains from eating and drinking from dawn to sunset. This goes on for an entire month, and the purpose is to attain God-consciousness… The fifth pillar is to make a pilgrimage to Mecca at least once in a person's lifetime if one is able. One benefit of the pilgrimage is that it unites Muslims from around the world.

Khalil emphasizes that many traditions exist in Islam. One tradition is to cleanse your body before prayer. "People typically wash up before they pray. The idea is that you're cleansing yourself of your sins. So, by the way, if you ever see a Muslim with their foot in the sink, now you know what that's about!"

Khalil then goes on to explain that Muslim holidays are big parts of worship services at the mosque:

There are two major holidays, and the first one comes after the month of fasting, Ramadan. The next one comes about two months and ten days later. This one is known as the Festival of Sacrifice. It commemorates the episode where Abraham is commanded to sacrifice his son Ishmael. In the end, he doesn't have to do that, but the point is that he showed he would do anything for God.

The latter holiday overlaps with the pilgrimage to Mecca, Saudi Arabia. Muslims from all over the world make the journey every year.

A COMMUNITY CENTER and a school are attached to the mosque. The school spans from pre-kindergarten to eighth grade. The children study regular American subjects, such as math and English, on top of Islamic readings and teachings. The school has some teachers who aren't Muslim, and Imam Mabrouk believes that diversity within the classroom creates a better learning environment.

Imam Mabrouk not only leads worship but also works as a counselor for members of the mosque. He's originally from Michigan, but he moved to California and then studied Islam for six years in Canada. At 23 years old, Imam Mabrouk is one of the youngest imams in Michigan. During his early years as an imam, his legitimacy was challenged because he was so young. He says that senior members of the mosque approached him asking, "Well, where did you find this? How do you know that's true?" But today, Imam Mabrouk finds joy in teaching everyone who once doubted him.

MORE THAN TEN years ago, the Islamic Center went through strife because of the tragic attacks on September 11, 2001. In the months that followed, the mosque was subject to drive-by gunfire. There were also people who ran into the mosque and confronted Muslims inside. Thankfully, no physical violence was reported during these confrontations.

Because of those incidents, local residents began to do more interfaith work, which is something that Khalil sees as a "silver lining" for East Lansing's religious community. Imam Mabrouk believes that interfaith work can bring together people who usually wouldn't speak to one another. "To be honest," he says:

> It was very difficult right after 9/11 for the first few years, but now I feel like people have come to understand Islam more. At the time, I was flying back-and-forth from Canada. I remember they gave me a really hard time at the border. It's not as bad now as it was before.

Imam Mabrouk has found some challenges in his position but is still happy that he came to East Lansing. He hadn't always considered becoming a faith leader, though. For a time, he says, "I wanted to be a chemist. I liked working in a laboratory, and I thought it was fun. But ultimately Islam is what I studied, and I always found my heart coming back to this. I've always enjoyed helping people and leading people."

He wants to see the mosque expand and continue to be an integral part of the area's growing Muslim community. "I'm trying to draw as many people as close to the mosque as possible."

12

We Are God Wrestlers
— Kehillat Israel, Lansing

By Yvonne Makidon, Ph.D., with photography by Olivia Hill

A T SUNDOWN ON Friday, October 18, Shabbat begins at Kehillat Israel, a Reconstructionist and Conservative synagogue housed in an old elementary school building a few miles south of downtown Lansing. This Sabbath features a children's service. A few families with young children meander into the sanctuary as a busy mom prepares the Oneg Shabbat—which means "Joy of the Sabbath"—in the kitchen.

Rabbi Michael Zimmerman welcomes the congregants while playing his guitar and singing in Hebrew. Children as young as 6 participate as much as they can. A 4-year-old moves closer to the rabbi, while others fidget near their parents.

During the service, colorfully sheathed Torahs—scrolls with the first five books of the Jewish Bible—are removed from the Ark. The families watch as the Torahs are paraded around the sanctuary by Rabbi Zimmerman and four children. Fifty minutes later, the service ends, and the congregants convene at the Oneg

Shabbat in the social hall.

Here, the congregants participate in a ceremony that thanks God for the wine and bread that nourish the body. Everyone receives a small plastic cup filled with red wine—children get grape juice—a prayer is sung in Hebrew and everyone drinks. The rabbi asks the children to lay their hands on the challah (Jewish braided egg bread) as a second prayer is offered. Led by the children, congregants tear off chunks and share the bread.

In a discussion afterwards about why Jews often mistrust outsiders, a young mother asserts, "Jews have been kicked out of everywhere!" She continues, "The Jewish people are survivors. They have been a community for thousands of years. We don't have priests because the Temple was torn down," referring to the Holy Temple in Jerusalem that was destroyed by the Romans. "We have rabbis. They are our teachers." Congregants speak about the importance of community in Kehillat Israel. One observes, "Being in a community keeps us strong. It is the reason why Jews are still here."

That sense of community is present on this Friday evening in mid-October. It gives these families a sense of belonging, of closeness and connection. From the prayers in Hebrew to the shared challah, there's a tangible sense of being part of something bigger than oneself.

———

AT 10 A.M. the following day, a second, more formal Shabbat service is celebrated. No children are present. Men and women wear tallitot (prayer shawls), and all of the men and some of the women wear kippot (skullcaps). Two types of books are used for worship: Hebrew-English prayer books and chumashim. The chumashim contain the five books of Moses and selections from the Prophets in Hebrew and English. Most prayers are sung in both languages, accompanied by guitar and hand-thumping.

There is great ceremony before the Torah reading. The large scroll is removed from the Ark and paraded around the sanctuary. The congregants touch the scroll as it passes—some use their prayer books, others use the edges of their prayer shawls and often kiss the edge of the shawls after they touch the Torah. After the Torah has passed around the sanctuary, it is removed from its ornate velvet sheath. It is set on a table that has been cleared with reverence, and it is carefully unrolled for the reading.

Reverence for the Torah is clear. Men and women read seven short excerpts from the Torah, an honor called an aliyah, which means "to go up." When the readings are completed, the scroll is ceremoniously lifted, re-tied and re-covered. It is then carried around the sanctuary for a second time and returned to the Ark. A velvet curtain is drawn to conceal it.

On this Saturday, a postmodern discussion takes place in which the congregants

Encased in the Holy Ark are the Torah scrolls.

enjoy asking big questions. They look forward to asking about God. They wrestle with what is found in the Torah. Such discussions are part of their heritage, "much like Jacob wrestles with the angel," one congregant explains. This questioning and curiosity defines them as a people, and as another congregant puts it, "We are God wrestlers."

Humor is a large part of their culture, and at a *kiddush* following the service, one congregant notes that "Jews feed people. This is important to us." Humor is a large part of their culture, and one congregant notes that "Jews are absurdists. This is how we survived." Again they pray before the drinking of the wine and the tearing of the challah.

This community welcomes outsiders and exhibits passion about its culture and beliefs. Rabbi Zimmerman says, "We are not sheep. Jews are individualists." When asked about misconceptions about Judaism, he replies, "We are not a church—we are a synagogue. Judaism is not based on belief, but rather on identity with the Jewish people and performance of at least some of its rituals and customs. Jewishness is not primarily a religion. It is one component of a way of life for a people, a history. 'Judaism' is a modern concept."

According to Rabbi Zimmerman, who has been at Kehillat Israel for ten years, there are about 120 families connected with the synagogue, and some of them have been here for multiple generations. The congregants value inclusivity, and they want others to know about them, their culture and their religious practices. Even so, he believes that Kehillat Israel is invisible in some ways locally.

As for his role in the synagogue, he says, "I work with wonderful people and get to be deeply involved in their lives." He studied family therapy at Oakland University and looks at the congregation "as a system," which is helpful when dealing with families within the community.

Rabbi Zimmerman understands that as part of Jewish practice, "individual members work to promote social justice within the community." He is actively involved with other local clergy and says that "educating our children has been a top priority."

In addition, he says, "People need to know there are different kinds of Judaism. We ask questions. The journey is exploration. We do what we can. We are survivors."

A classroom window displays the Hebrew alphabet.

13

The Church Really Stresses Family

— Lake Lansing Baptist Church, East Lansing

By Katlin Barth with photography by Breanna Bishop

I N THE PAMPHLET given to each attendee, the order of service is straightforward, just like Lake Lansing Baptist Church's pastor, Robert Grimwood, who describes the church as conservative and traditional. Lake Lansing Baptist differentiates itself from other churches by being more specific in its beliefs. For example, before an individual becomes an official member, he or she receives a sixty-one-page manual written by Pastor Grimwood that outlines every aspect of the church. Before becoming a pastor, Pastor Grimwood thought the beliefs of a church should be clearly defined so that people are aware of what they are joining. The manual reflects this approach.

The congregants reflect the church's personality through their Sunday dress. Most of the men wear button-down shirts, and the women wear dress pants or skirts. These men and women bring their families with them to services. Most of the families have children, and a few have grandparents sitting with them. It's a small

Pastor Robert Grimwood
has led Lake Lansing
Baptist Church for two
decades in a conservative,
straightforward fashion.

church, with members who value harmony and understand and accept one another no matter one's age. "The church really stresses family" and includes many three-generational families, says Pastor Grimwood.

Its homeschool cooperative, Robert Raikes Academy, educates children through seventh grade. The church believes in the benefits of integrating the older generation with the younger, so two to three times per year, the children visit with Caleb's Kin, a senior ministry that meets every second Tuesday of the month. The children often sing or perform skits, puppet shows or plays for the older group. They share a meal or a learning opportunity and listen to stories and play games with the seniors. In return, the elders advise the children on how to act and how to serve God and the church.

There are many other opportunities for members of different ages to interact. For example, Prayer Moms and Prayer Dads anonymously match "parents" with children in the congregation, and those "parents" give gifts to their "children" every three months. "As our children are growing up, we want to have an active interest in their lives," says Pastor Grimwood. "I have a feeling that it will have a good effect because you will remember those people with fondness, no matter where you end up."

Another group, FUN (Fellowship, Unity and Nutrition), hosts seasonal events that combine food and activities such as games, movies, sledding, pumpkin-carving and other family-oriented fun. A group called Men's Timeout, which enables men in the congregation to spend time together, holds events such as fishing trips and sporting activities. The women spend time together during the Ladies' Bible Studies and at events such as Zehnder's Snowfest in Frankenmuth, Michigan, and shopping trips to Birch Run, Michigan, and Shipshewana, Indiana.

Lake Lansing Baptist does leave its congregants a few free weekends each month with no church events so they can focus on their own families. Pastor Grimwood says he doesn't want members to be so busy with church activities that they forget about their lives at home. And should problems arise between a couple, he and his wife, Judy, offer counseling. He wants members of the church to be generous and helpful to people with needs. "Individuals should have an impact on their community," he says, and he believes that one of his primary roles is to prepare members to demonstrate their faith. "Our first and foremost goal is to represent Jesus Christ. We are to feed the hungry and give water to the thirsty and give clothing to the naked."

During this Sunday's service, he discusses being charitable within each individual's limits. He doesn't expect members to give if they're financially unable to. He does expect them to care for their family's needs first and then donate if they can. He describes, for example, how to assist others when there is money to do so, but sometimes those funds aren't there. "People in the community call for help, and the church helps where we can. We do what we can and that's all we can do. Churches can't meet all the needs."

FOR MOST OF his life, Pastor Grimwood didn't envision himself as a minister, and he used to tell people, "That person has to be crazy to be a pastor." He remembers how, at the church he attended as a child, congregants who didn't like the pastors often scared them off or discouraged them so they'd leave.

While in Bible college, he became fond of a woman who would, against his prediction, marry him. That woman told him that she thought God was calling her to become a pastor's wife. That made him think that perhaps they weren't meant to be a couple, and he told her, "I'd be crazy to be a pastor." Yet they remained together as he became a teacher and then a principal, and at one point, joked that when he turned 40 he'd think about changing careers. On his fortieth birthday, his wife reminded him of the joke he'd made earlier in their relationship. Other people also had suggested that he become ordained, and when he did, a friend coaxed him into sending out résumés to see what would happen.

At the time, Lake Lansing Baptist was looking for a pastor. It called him to preach and later to become a candidate for the opening. He officiated at worship even though he wasn't interested in the job. That same night, however, 93 percent of the members voted to hire him. As a result, he's been at the church for the past twenty years.

He initially served because he felt a sense of duty, but he grew to love his work. "God has been good to me. It's a very good church, and we've got good people. There is no doubt in my mind this is where God wanted me."

14

A Community within the Community

— Liberty Christian Church, Lansing

By Yvonne Makidon, Ph.D., with photography by Andrea Raby

SUN COVERS THE arriving worshippers as cars slowly fill the parking lot. It's a perfect fall morning—the kind that fools Midwesterners into believing that summer is here to stay.

Liberty Christian Church is on the east side of Lansing on a downtown street lined with businesses that are closed on this late Sunday morning. The back and side of the building blend in with the surrounding neighborhood, and the front faces a wide thoroughfare. The entry doors are wide open, and a few early worshippers busy themselves with readying for the service. To the left of the open doors, streaks of sunlight illuminate the sanctuary with its twenty-foot ceilings and echoing music as the worship band warms up with contemporary songs. Youthful, casually-dressed singers are alongside the instrumentalists. One young man has tattoos running up one arm.

A man carrying a cane and dressed in black introduces himself as "Malcolm." He's been a pastor at the church for

Dr. Malcolm Magee makes announcements to his congregation.

twenty-one years and now opens and closes the weekly service. Dr. Malcolm Magee is also an associate professor of history at Michigan State University and is transitioning from being a minister to a professor. For now, he straddles both worlds. A new associate minister is in place but out of town for training.

The parishioners filter in. There are people of various ages dressed in everything from jeans to suits. One lone woman sits in the back row, seemingly a regular worshipper. Wearing a bright orange bandana and carrying a tightly packed blue bag, she clutches a tennis ball throughout the service. Dr. Magee describes her as struggling with mental health problems. She seems content, and those around her greet her affectionately.

Greeters hover at the rear door of the sanctuary and dispense church fliers, occasionally hugging people as they file in. Families with young children sit in the rear, while others move to the front of the sanctuary. Children under the age of 5 run and play, and no one seems to mind as their energy adds to the lively atmosphere.

As the worship team continues to play and sing, more people fill the sanctuary. Close to 100 people begin to clap and sway and dance to the lively music. Everyone gets involved, and moms hover over their young charges who are busily displaying their enthusiasm in the moment. While the worship team prepares the hearts of the congregants, Dr. Magee invites children and teachers to leave for Sunday school lessons. As the children bounce through the sanctuary doors, a sense of seriousness descends.

Announcements are made. In one family, another grandchild was born this past week. Additional volunteers are needed after the service to prepare sack lunches for Advent House, a local organization that helps Greater Lansing's underserved population and is supported by a coalition of congregations in the area. Liberty Christian supplies eighty sack lunches each month to Advent House, and today is its volunteers' turn to prepare them.

After the announcements, the congregants are invited into the next room for tea or coffee and are instructed to bring their beverages back into the sanctuary to hear the morning's lesson. After everyone returns, a prayer is said and an offering is gathered into brown wicker baskets.

A lay speaker begins with a sermon on needs versus wants. Food and water and shelter are needs—just ask the people at Advent House. As young children, we depend completely on our parents to meet our needs. We then grow toward independence. Finally, as we age and become frailer, we once again need someone to care for our bodies. The speaker lifts the congregants a little higher, talking about God and how God's people should want what God wants, not be driven by their own needs.

During the sermon, congregants occasionally murmur agreement or echo similar sentiments. The heads nodding in agreement seem to suggest that everyone in the sanctuary is on board with the message. After the sermon, communion is offered. The congregants file out of their pews to receive the bread and wine. Gluten-free wafers are also available. Another song plays, and people leave.

Volunteers rush into the kitchen and dining hall to make eighty lunches. Bread slices are lined up on a long folding table. Some workers efficiently slap fixings onto the bread, while others in the kitchen divvy up the remaining portions of the lunches. Brown paper sacks are arrayed, awaiting their contents.

TWO DAYS AFTER the service, Dr. Magee talks about the church's history. Liberty Christian started as a college group on Michigan State's campus in the 1980s, and some founders still belong. Although the church is non-denominational, Dr. Magee comes from a different

Congregants raise their hands and close their eyes in praise as the band plays contemporary worship music.

background. He grew up on the West Coast in a family of Quakers. He married at 19, started his religious studies early in adulthood, spent many years in various churches and became known as "a fixer." How did he end up in Lansing? "I came here to fix Liberty and stayed."

In August 2000, when he was a minister and an MSU graduate student, tragedy befell him. He was parked on the side of Interstate 496 assisting his 22-year-old daughter whose car had broken down. He'd called a tow truck to take her car to a repair shop. When he left his vehicle to talk with the tow truck driver, he was hit by a car that had spun out of control at 70 mph. He spent the next two excruciating months in the hospital. The accident cost him his left leg below the knee. He spent the next four years in pain, in and out of a wheelchair. During that time, he went on to earn his PhD.

Dr. Magee doesn't sound bitter. Even though he has a prosthetic leg and still experiences pain, he believes the accident was important for his development because it made him "more empathetic for people" and gave him insight into other people's battles. Before the accident, he didn't consider himself a bad person, but "I was a person who did not understand."

This life-changing event impacted his ministry as well. He sees the world differently now, which is something essential for a church like Liberty Christian where people who are different can come together in a safe space and love one another.

THERE ARE TWO groups at Liberty Christian: "those under 30 and everyone else." The congregants include professors, graduate students, a member of the city council and street people who show up on occasion. They also include General Motors autoworkers and people from other countries.

The church has a resource room with clothing and appliances for those in need. "Our neighborhood is full of young families. Student rentals are cheap, and other working-class people who are in the low-income range can afford to live there." Dr. Magee believes his congregation is more racially diverse than some other churches in the Lansing area, adding that the members of Liberty Christian "want to reach out and make the world better."

There is a political split, Dr. Magee notes, among local congregations: the religious right and the left. "Most churches gravitate one way or the other. We try and maneuver through this and create a place where people from different political views can love each other." In a 2008 article in *Lansing City Pulse*, he talks about being labeled "the left hand of God." Traditionally and historically, the Church at large has stood on the side of social justice issues such as women's rights, abolition, child labor and equitable distribution of income. Dr. Magee believes that "Christians and the churches they belong to have a moral obligation to help and become involved in social justice issues and in politics when appropriate."

Being a historian also helps him view religion and people from a unique perspective. When he came to Liberty Christian, "I was the only Democrat in the church," but the ratio of Democrats and Republicans has probably shifted to 50/50 now. "This goes beyond my influence. The Republican economic message has collided with the teachings of Jesus." His personal philosophy is: "We need a mental health system and a just society. Our people— under the age of 40—are economically on the left. So is it public or private means that best serve the poor?" He insists that it doesn't matter to him how the poor get served—he "just wants to see Jesus's work get done. Churches always provoke reactions. People's inner turmoil always focuses on God." When asked how the community views Liberty Christian, he responds, "The community would see us differently based on their own experiences and who within the church they are connected with. Our church fits in the community. We have a generous, educated congregation. My conservative congregants have compassion for people."

Liberty Christian "is a community within the community. People will drag you into their homes, their lives and include you."

Dr. Magee sees his role as helping people to get along, as well as "keeping people generous to each other" and to the mission of the church. His belief is also reflected in Liberty Christian's vision statement, which says the church wishes to "train a community of people who seek the kingdom of God first and His righteousness, disregarding personal cost or sacrifice." In twenty years, he continues, the church should be doing the same thing —"doing good." He feels some loss about leaving his church leadership role to become a professor, but "I technically died the day of the accident. The accident made me content with where I am at." Before he lost his leg, he was angry and experiencing an inner crisis in which "faith and reason were battling it out." He now believes that faith and reason are friends. "Certainty is the opposite of faith—not doubt." For him, doubt and faith are friends, and faith and reason are friends too.

The constant pain is a reminder of that most difficult time in his life. "I'm not bitter. Losing a leg is a grief response, like losing a family member." From the hospital he phoned the woman who was driving that car on that fateful day, and he told her, "'It was an accident and I am okay.' After my dark moment, I forgave her. Someone is out there who has changed my life." After a brief pause he adds, "Faith had me—I did not have faith."

A woman raises her hand in worship as her daughter clings to her. Children are included in the worship part of the service before Sunday school.

15

God Was Passionately Pursuing Me

— Mount Hope Church, Lansing

By Tyler Hendon with photography by Cara Oteto and Jordan Jennings

A MASSIVE STRUCTURE accompanied by a football-field-sized parking lot makes Mount Hope Church one of the biggest churches in Lansing. It's located on South Creyts Road, about fifteen minutes from Michigan State University's campus. The flags of many nations fly over the entrance. Greeters stroll around the church assisting visitors in seating, parking and other matters. A sense of unity and acceptance can be felt.

The worship services begin promptly at 8:00 a.m., 9:30 a.m. and 11:30 a.m. Lights fill the room while mounted cameras swing around the sanctuary, catching every angle of the experience. The congregants rise swiftly when the music begins. They clap and wave their hands in rhythm while the music plays amid positive energy. Every aspect of the service seems to encourage fellowship. After the singing concludes, congregants happily high-five their neighbors and share smiles.

In the pews are pamphlets about the process for becoming

a member of the church. The pamphlets encourage visitors to "Begin, Belong and Become" in the hope that they will become members too.

The first half of the service is instructional as Pastor Kevin Berry preaches about tithing and the importance of giving back to the church. He calls for people to be "clothed in love," meaning that they should surround themselves with loved ones while using their energy to give to others. He also urges them to "love outrageously" and to make the Lansing community a better place. "You'll never expect God to be kind to you if you don't know how kind He is," he says.

Reverend Joseph Mead, the church's communications manager, says working for Mount Hope is much more than just a job for him. "I've experienced God and I feel like He has put me together in the experiences I've had. There is a difference between a career and a calling. This message is vital, it's historical and it's eternal."

Mount Hope has places for its many congregants to meet, relax, eat and, most importantly, worship. There are rooms dedicated to greeting visitors, as well as a wing dedicated to the youth ministry. Reverend Mead feels that Mount Hope, or "The Hope," invests greatly in its youth ministry because members want their congregation to produce positive people. "Children are absolutely vital. They're the next future educators, the next business-people and the future leaders of the world. They're integrated into the service. We're really a family-based church. We're trying to cultivate healthy relationships."

Reverend Mead, who grew up in nearby Waverly, has worked directly for Mount Hope Church for almost ten years now. He spent some time away from Lansing but has been involved with the church in one way or another for twenty years. Most recently, he took his two children to Mount Hope's annual Hallelujah Party, which drew more than 4,000 people to the church for a safe and scare-free event for the whole family.

Reverend Mead says The Hope has made him a better human being over time. As a teenager on a winter retreat, he had what he sees as a breakthrough in his life:

> I remember going on a youth retreat when I was about 17 years old. During the retreat, we studied the Bible and just answered tough questions over three days. I was allowed to seek God on the retreat. An experience with God that is difficult to put into words led me know that Jesus was real. It wasn't just words on a page anymore. I realized that God was passionately pursuing me. I've never been disappointed since.

Despite all its success, Mount Hope hasn't been without challenges. One such challenge, in February 2012, was the transition from Pastor Dave Williams to Pastor Kevin Berry. "I think transitioning from one pastor to the next was a little tough," Reverend Mead

Pastor Kevin Berry prays for the community to experience God's love.

says. "Some people may recognize and identify with the old pastor. The pastoral transition was planned for about five years. Often churches lose members and giving decreases when this happens." He believes that good planning played a huge part in the church's continuing success.

Reaching college students has posed some challenges as well, he says. "Students have a really hectic lifestyle. At that time of life you're pretty much entrenched in education. I think recently we are doing a lot better in reaching college students, but I think in the history of Mount Hope it's been difficult."

WHEN ASKED WHERE he sees Mount Hope being in the next decade, Reverend Mead predicts that it will grow exponentially. "We expect 30 percent growth and opportunities to reach more people through live streaming and more video projection."

Mount Hope plans to expand and move further into the Lansing community as it gets older, and the leadership believes that teaching their congregants simple, effective lessons helps them thrive. Reverend Mead explains:

We really want to teach the Gospel in a practical way: how we raise our kids, talk to our kids and how we stay married. I believe this is what helps us strengthen our families. Scripture can be very complex and very deep, so we break it down practically. Pastor Kevin makes sure everything he teaches connects.

MOUNT HOPE ENGAGES in multiple community service and humanitarian causes. Pastor Berry says congregants must be mobile when looking to affect homelessness and poverty: "I don't believe there is a limit to the ways we are able to share God's message." On top of financially supporting congregants on mission trips, it supports more than 300 ministries and missionaries in more than 100 countries. Mount Hope provides free lunches and activities for people interested in becoming members. It also has groups for anyone looking to learn more about the Christian faith and supports ministries in Lansing.

Mount Hope recently invested in Pastor Billy Graham's thirty-minute program "The Cross" and donated to the Billy Graham Evangelistic Association to get the program on television. Mount Hope was successful in obtaining airtime for the program on CBS and ABC throughout mid-Michigan.

The program features Grammy Award-winning hip-hop artist Lecrae and singer Lacey Sturm. It tells their stories of hardship and what made them become Christians. Pastor Berry encourages members to watch the film together and open their homes to anyone wishing to view it. He describes the program as "one of the most compelling presentations of the Gospel I have ever seen."

Pastor Billy Graham is an extremely influential evangelist who has preached in front of hundreds of thousands of people around the globe during his lifetime. His message is that God loves everyone and is willing to forgive. In the program, he asks viewers to "bring about a renewal of faith" and to humbly thank God for their blessings.

"The Cross" sells for $15.99 through the association's website, but Mount Hope gives it out for free. Reverend Mead calls this a blessing because it spreads the church's message as far as possible.

Ultimately, Pastor Berry wants Mount Hope to fit into one of his favorite parts of Scripture, Ephesians 4:16: "He makes the whole body fit together perfectly. As each part does its own special work, it helps the other parts grow, so that the whole body is healthy, growing, and full of love." He believes this is "God's blueprint for the local church."

Dozens of countries' flags line Mount Hope Church's driveway, signaling the church's passion for community and global outreach.

16

We Embrace the Tension
— The Peoples Church, East Lansing

By Joshua Anderson with photography by Brittany Holmes

A NICELY DRESSED elderly man stands in the doorway. A father with two young daughters walks down the hallway toward the man, but his progress is slowed as his children walk this way and that, anywhere but straight. When they reach the threshold of the chapel, the usher hands them a brochure for the day's worship service. The small room is already mostly filled, so getting to an empty seat in a pew requires stepping past one or two singing congregants. One moves for the late arrivals without protest, his hymnal held open in front of him with one hand, a thumb pressed against the crease of the pages and the arch of his fingers supporting the spine. The father of the two children grabs a hymnal and flips through it until he finds number fifty-four, "Make a Joyful Noise to God!" Then the family joins in the chorus.

The morning's 8:30 worship service is a prelude to a much larger gathering in the church's spacious sanctuary two hours later. About forty people attend the early service, but The Peoples Church is filled with more than ten times as many congregants for the 10:30 a.m. worship.

The chapel is a cozy, comforting place that takes up but a small portion of the building's massive floor space, complementing the many other rooms used throughout the week for worship and study. Its official title is the "McCune Chapel," named after a beloved pastor who started his thirty-two-year ministry at the church almost 100 years ago. The chapel isn't the only room named in honor of an individual: With a history going back as far as The Peoples Church's, more than a few members have served the congregation with enthusiasm long enough to be honored with a dedication. A basement room is devoted to the rich history of the building and the building that came before it. Pictures line the walls documenting the church's past, as do shelves of publications by members. Most of them, including *The Peoples Church Oral History*, *Celebrating Our Heritage* and *Legacy of Love: the Interior Design and Sacred Art of The Peoples Church*, were published in 2007, a full century after its founding.

But Pastor Andrew Pomerville, who is delivering the sermon today, is so new to the church that his name isn't mentioned in *A Century of Ecumenical Worship, Education and Service: The History of The Peoples Church of East Lansing Michigan*, which isn't the first or second but the *third* narrative account of its history. The church's leadership took him on as pastor just two years ago. At first, he was overwhelmed by the size of the church and the enormity of the role offered to him. He initially turned down the invitation, but several months later the church approached him again. "'We know you're going to make a ton of mistakes,'" Pastor Pomerville recalls being told. "'You will probably fail an awful lot here.'" He pauses. "And I remember there was never a 'but'—they just left it hanging out there," he chuckles. The interviewer continued: "'And when you do, we'll continue to love you and support you and we hope to grow with you.'"

The topic of the sermon today is thankfulness. Pastor Pomerville describes the way young children are able to accept compliments gratefully without reservation, but notes how that quality is lost as they grow older. A teenager whose drawing attracts praise may point out its imperfections, and an adult may respond to a commendation by commenting how it's "no big deal." But sometimes, he tells the worshippers, "you're welcome" is the best response possible.

The exact title of his sermon is "Um, Thanks. I Guess?" but on the pulpit he sounds confident. "Thank you," he says sincerely to the congregation, hoping they'll accept his gratitude as children would. Thank you, he seems to be saying, because you, the church, deserve it. Thank you, friends, for the experiences you've allowed me to have as your pastor.

Pastor Andrew Pomerville talks about the importance of being thankful for what we have and how life is a continuously complex endeavor.

PASTOR POMERVILLE IS proud to say the church has grown more energetic since he's come on board. It's not a knock on leaders of the past, he insists, but rather an indication of where the congregation is now. "We're very, very accepting of families at this point. Kids didn't used to have a role in worship—we've changed that so that it's revolving around them." As the church bulletin says, "A crying baby is a wonderful noise," but the two young girls accompanying their father this morning don't put that maxim to the test.

Of course, being the senior pastor of a multi-denominational church—not non-denominational, he emphasizes—comes with its own unique set of challenges. So unique, in fact, that The Peoples Church is often called "The Great Experiment."

As the story goes, the idea for the church was born from the ponderings of four professors at what used to be known as the Michigan Agricultural College. It was the early 1900s, and they often met under a willow and discussed the lack of a Protestant church in their small but growing community, a place that would eventually be chartered

The multi-denominational church offers many areas for its members to pray.

as East Lansing in 1907. No single denomination in the area was populous enough to support a congregation of its own, so the professors toyed with the concept of a multi-denominational church, an unheard-of idea at the time.

From the start, the church had strong ties to the nearby university. In its 1924 Articles of Agreement, the church specifically named ministry to the students and faculty of the Agricultural College as its mission. An early leader of the church was also the college president. Michigan State University, as the college came to be called, is still intimately connected to The Peoples Church, which "revolves around MSU's calendar." The scheduling and outcome of sporting events influences the attendance at the services, Pastor Pomerville says with a laugh.

When The Peoples Church was officially established on December 8, 1907, it had eighty-three members representing eleven denominations. Today, the church aligns itself

The featured stained glass in the Peoples Church is the backdrop to the front of the church and spans the length of two stories.

with four: the Presbyterian Church (U.S.A.), the United Church of Christ, the American Baptist Church and the United Methodist Church. To Pastor Pomerville, this means, "We're attached to these four. You're a member of all those four. We have the accountability of all four, but at the same time we're trying to blend them together." In fact, there's a requirement that all of the clergy staff come from different denominations. "Necessarily, we won't agree on everything," explains Pastor Pomerville. For example, Pastor Pomerville, a Presbyterian, has a different standpoint on the baptism of babies than the church's newest associate pastor, who comes from the Church of Christ.

Even so, the congregation appreciates the sense of diversity that stems from such disagreements. "We embrace the tension," Pastor Pomerville explains. At its core, The

Members of the church often donate their time and resources to the church, such as the materials and time used to create this scene at the front of the church.

Peoples Church holds that Jesus Christ is Lord, but "anything after that is fair game and up for debate." Doctrine, social policy, social justice issues, appropriate worship attire and the like are not nearly as important.

What *is* important to the congregation is staying relevant. Pastor Pomerville admits that he sometimes questions whether anyone would care if The Peoples Church were to disappear. After all, at its founding, it was the only place of its kind in the area, but now there are hundreds of nearby houses of worship competing for attendees. The pastor cringes. He hates the concept of churches "competing," as if congregants are paying customers who expect something in return for their attendance.

Even with the many alternatives in the area, The Peoples Church has grown substantially in the past few years. This is despite the transient nature of most college community churches, as attendees tend to move away after they finish their degrees. Pastor Pomerville is "blown away" by how many alumni remain in the Lansing area after graduation.

Nationwide, Christian churches have faced diminishing attendance since the 1950s and 1960s. The success of The Peoples Church in fighting this trend may be due to its revitalized look toward the church as an institution. The old model of church, he explains, was that people joined a congregation because they already believed what was taught there. But that's antithetical to how Christianity started. "The early church was all about involving people, inviting them to dinners, helping their neighbors and creating this great family atmosphere and community, and then belief and doctrine were developed." Somewhere along the line, that switched. Printed at the top of the church's Sunday handout is a line reflecting the inclusive, accepting spirit of The Peoples Church: "Whether you are young or old, rich or poor, doubtful or hopeful, no matter where you are in your faith journey, YOU are welcome here."

For The Peoples Church, "here" isn't always the building itself. "We should be a church without walls," Pastor Pomerville says, meaning a church out in the community, living its teachings both inside the chapel and out.

"Pick a type of cause or a giving place—we see our people there." Not all such causes and giving places are sponsored by The Peoples Church, but its members show up just the same. Service, to these congregants, isn't just about the time and money they contribute to their church, but also about what they give to the world at large.

Infrequent attendance doesn't bother Pastor Pomerville, who is perfectly happy to see members busy in the community. Parents should feel no guilt in attending their kids' dance classes; children should feel no shame in skipping Sunday service in lieu of soccer practice. Nobody should ever feel like they aren't a "good Christian" for pursuing any number of passions or activities outside of the church. "Whether you come here every week or once every four years, when you're here you should feel like you're part of our family."

As the early morning service concludes, congregants empty out of the chapel into the entrance hall. A table with coffee is set up, and the worshippers waste no time filling their cups.

Pastor Pomerville stands at the entrance of the foyer, shaking hands and greeting members as they pass. Some depart after exchanging a few words with him while others make their way toward the tables placed around the room, striking up conversations with friends they haven't seen in a week—or in years.

Suddenly, the voice of a woman comes from the direction of the pastor. Her volume and sincerity cut through every other discussion. All that can be heard from afar are two words before her speech dips back down to a conversational level: "Thank you!" she says to Pastor Pomerville, shaking his hand heartily.

The Peoples Church is available for people to come in and pray multiple times throughout the week.

Old masonry from the original building is visible throughout the building.

17

Pilgrim Congregational Welcomes You!

— Pilgrim Congregational United Church of Christ, Lansing

By Duygu Kanver with photography by Dylan Sowle

"WELCOME," SAYS THE elderly woman in a burgundy jacket and matching skirt as congregants enter the church through the back door. By the sincere look on her face, her smile and her two-handed handshake, one strongly feels that she means it—that people are welcome at Pilgrim Congregational United Church of Christ.

Welcoming is indeed the right word to use to define this church. The big red sign on Pennsylvania Avenue is proof of this. It reads, "Pilgrim Congregational United Church of Christ Welcomes You." Right below the underlined "you"—which gives passersby the impression that it addresses them specifically—are three logos. There's the rainbow flag that symbolizes the LGBT movement; the well-known blue wheelchair symbol that shows that the building is accessible for people with disabilities; and a large black-on-red comma, the symbol of the "God is still speaking" campaign of the United Church of Christ. The campaign

Pastor Peter Robinson's sermons focus on the church's primary messages of acceptance of all people and respect for and encouragement of one another.

theme is: "No matter who you are, or where you are on life's journey, you're welcome here." And Pilgrim Congregational, a member of the United Church of Christ, embraces this philosophy.

In the long, spacious hallway, congregants gather in groups of three, five or a few more. Most congregants are over the age of 60 or 65. As they greet one another, they talk about this sunny Sunday morning and how it's one of the last warm days of the year. It is indeed pleasant. With a temperature of 70 degrees outside on this mid-October day, congregants don't need their coats. Older members wear their Sunday best, while a few younger adults have chosen jeans and nice tops. A blind transgender woman walks by in a denim skirt and a rainbow-colored pair of knee-high socks. There's no dress code at Pilgrim Congregational.

As congregants walk toward the sanctuary a few minutes before 10 o'clock, Norma

Bauer, one of the regulars of the church, notes how her friend looks nice in that skirt suit, and adds, "As usual." Bauer is one of the youngest members even though she's in her mid-60s. She is one of the newer members as well: she's been attending the church for the last two years and became a member last year—but seems to know everyone at the service.

In fact, everyone knows one another here. A young visitor, as she looks for a seat in the sanctuary, certainly doesn't go unnoticed by a group of congregants gathered near the entrance. One asks how she is doing today. Another, an elderly man, cracks a joke and makes her smile. And Bauer doesn't hide her curiosity as she remarks, "You sure must be new to us, huh?" They all treat her with such sincerity that it seems as if they've known her for a long time.

BY 10 O'CLOCK, everyone is seated in the sanctuary. It is not big and elaborate but rather simple and warm. The faint smell of the wood fills the sanctuary. The dark brown color of the wooden pews, windows and frame of the room contrasts well with the white brick walls. Daylight comes in through the stained glass. The nine windows in the sanctuary are decorated with stained glass figures. Some depict the history of the church, some are about Michigan and some have images that represent Christianity. Each is beautiful, but the windows labeled "Good Shepherd" and "Jesus Christ" are especially meaningful because they were moved here from Pilgrim Congregational's old building, which burned down in 1917.

The Messengers, one of the four music ministries at Pilgrim Congregational, performs the opening music. Directly above the pulpit where the Messengers sing hangs a large projector screen. The lyrics are on the screen for the congregants to read.

In my Father's house, they never close the door.
In my Father's house, there's love and compassion.
In my Father's house, there's always room for more.

"In My Father's House," a Christian country song with a catchy tune, is one of a few songs written specifically for Pilgrim Congregational by Randy Roy, a local singer and songwriter. It emphasizes the welcoming nature of God, His house and the church. According to the program booklet handed to the congregants, today is Accessibility Sunday, a time to welcome people with disabilities and appreciate the unique abilities that God gives all His people.

When you do this to them,
You do this to me.
When you hold somebody's hand,
Help the blind to see.

This second song, "When You Do This to Them," delivers the "message in music,"

Stained glass windows in the sanctuary with religious images and symbols

according to the program booklet. The lyrics are the perfect fit for today's theme. After the song, Pastor Peter Robinson talks about this theme of the day during children's time. As he sits on the steps of the pulpit with two little kids, he explains what a disability is and tells them how they should be helpful and welcoming toward people with disabilities: "Jesus welcomed everyone, and so should we."

As parents see their children off to the Sunday school downstairs, Pastor Robinson gives his sermon on accessibility. One can feel how pleased the congregants are as

Congregants and members of the choir greet one another.

he speaks about the accessible structure of their building and their plans to improve it. Pastor Robinson's sermon doesn't take long. After fifteen minutes, he gives the floor to someone who has a better say on the subject—Laura Hall of ADAPT Michigan. Sitting in a wheelchair, she presents ADAPT's statewide and nationwide plans for helping people with disabilities overcome obstacles. After Hall's remarks, the congregants pray together with Pastor Robinson, marking the end of the Sunday service. The congregants then meet in the hall to have refreshments and to catch up with one another. After a lot of talking and eating together, they leave one by one, promising to see one another on Wednesday for the LGB-What? group discussion.

EVERY WEDNESDAY, GROUP discussions are held on intriguing topics that may concern devoted Christians. These group talks are food-for-thought sessions for participating

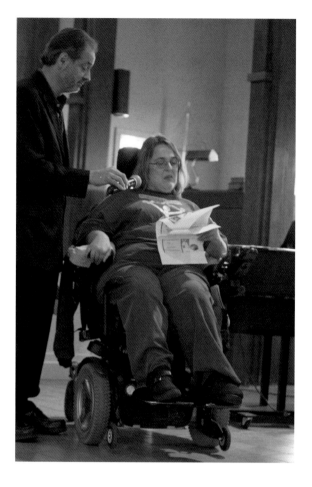

Pastor Mike Cooper holds the microphone as Laura Hall speaks on behalf of her ADAPT Michigan group as part of the church's Accessibility Sunday program.

congregants. Discussions about Halloween, visions of heaven and pagan roots of current beliefs are examples of the compelling topics for upcoming Wednesday nights.

The Wednesday that follows Accessibility Sunday is part two of the transgender discussion. Even the title, LGB-What? is enough to intrigue the audience, and the discussion itself is a mind-opener. About twenty congregants from ages 30 to more than 70 sit in a circle. A member named Abby distributes a fun and informative handout titled "The Genderbread Person" that discusses definitions of gender. Mike Cooper, the junior pastor, Abby and her wife Becky moderate the discussion.

Abby used to be Adam.

Abby and Becky married in Pilgrim Congregational not long ago but in the first few months of marriage, Adam discovered her true self and decided to become "she." After long and painstaking therapies and medical processes—a period known as the transitioning phase—Adam became Abby, and Becky has always been there for her. They didn't break up—in fact, they are happy as a couple and strong enough to moderate the LGB-What? discussion together.

Sure, some members could not welcome the transition instantly, and the two pastors received so much criticism about it that Pastor Robinson delivered a sermon on the topic to resolve the conflict within the church community. Some congregants felt "insulted and assaulted" by Abby's transition, and some thought the transition happened way too quickly without enough time for other members to get used to the "situation." Pastor Robinson says:

> I likened it to a person who's been in prison for twenty years, and you ask them to wait another month so the community can get used to the idea of that person being out. It's just like you want to be free. You want to be out. And that's the way, I believe, Abby felt about it.

He says the ones who objected did so because of their lack of knowledge. They didn't know who a transgender person is and how the term differs from many other terms about gender definitions.

That's why they hold such discussions at Pilgrim Congregational: to inform congregants so that they will welcome all people and respect their differences.

Having resolved that conflict, the members of the congregation are gladly participating in the discussion. Heterosexual participants, especially the older ones, are understanding, though still not very familiar with the topic. The discussion goes on like a Q&A session: members are introduced to the basics of being transgender, and they ask both Abby and Becky about their experiences. Other transgender congregants jump in and reflect on some of those questions. There isn't any disapproval in the room. In a positive and open manner, adults of all ages and all sexual orientations discuss an issue that is debated across the world.

"PEOPLE JUST LIKE each other here. People respect each other's differences and work things out when a problem arises. We are welcoming and affirming, and we live up to that. I am so proud of our members, really proud of them," says Bauer, the relatively new member, and one can read it in her eyes. What she says about her church is what makes Pilgrim Congregational United Church of Christ worth being a part of.

18

From the Rising of the Sun
— The Presbyterian Church of Okemos

By RJ Wolcott with photography by Elizabeth Izzo

ADAPTING TO AN ever-changing society is a challenge for any religious institution. How does a church bolster its ranks while remaining beloved by longtime members? Pastors and congregants cannot simply bury their history under a shiny new coat of paint every few years without the risk of losing their identity, while those on the other end of the spectrum cannot hope to stimulate young families and first-timers with long-abandoned moral platitudes.

Even with this unending struggle, the Presbyterian Church of Okemos stands tall, perched alongside a road that weaves travelers past numerous churches. What makes this one special? How does it grapple with these difficult queries? For the Reverend Dr. Robert Carlson, who has been a pastor for more than thirty years including seventeen spent in Okemos, the answer is providing a place where worshippers can enter and feel welcome.

The Reverend Dr. Robert Carlson is reflected in a framed painting of the Norwegian cathedral where his grandmother was baptized.

Walking through the church's main doors, visitors are greeted with a meticulously carved wooden shepherd carrying a sheep from his flock. In the 1980s, Father Bohdan Kosicki, who served a Roman Catholic parish in St. Clair Shores and entered religious art shows in the Lansing area, carved the "Good Shepherd" from driftwood found on the shores of Lake Superior. It was his way of protesting the military conflicts the United States was involved in at the time. The statue, now adorning the entryway, has cracked and grayed over the years but still exudes intrigue for the children and visitors who examine the figure as they meander about before the service. The subtle, featureless figure guides his sheep and demonstrates resilience, and according to Reverend Carlson, is a poignant and continuing symbol for the church.

Adjacent to the statue, the main worship hall is flooded with congregants attending Sunday's 10 a.m. service. Last-minute arrivals wriggle their way into the few available pews on the far side. Middle section seats appear highly coveted: with row after row of

The choir leads
the congregation
in a hymn.

congregants packed shoulder-to-shoulder as they sing the morning's opening hymn. High white walls enclose the vast oval sanctuary, which seats up to 400 worshippers on holidays such as Christmas and Easter. The deep oak-stained benches creak as worshippers rise and sit throughout the service, alternating between hymnals, the Bible and the week's printed materials. A vast rainbow tapestry wraps the communion table, radiating vibrantly as Reverend Carlson takes to the pulpit.

Upon reading the materials provided, visitors begin to understand how much goes on day to day at the Presbyterian Church of Okemos. Events throughout the week keep volunteers and members busy with Bible studies, choir practice and a cornucopia of dinners, brunches and sit-downs. Worshippers are invited to classes after the service as well as to activities for children from preschool to senior high. Before Reverend Carlson begins his message, he takes time to list the varied happenings around the church. The congregation silently reads along or nods with him. There's a swell of admiration for involved members as he expresses appreciation for all their hard work.

There are seasonal events and traditions listed, such as the yearly chili cook-off where mid-Michigan residents compete to make the best chili or simply sample others' offerings. There is promotion of events for teens and young adults, an important demographic for any congregation. Various food donation projects are underway as leaves become brittle and descend in cascades of crimson and copper. Thanksgiving food baskets, which are given to needy families in the community, swell with donations. An Evening of Lessons and Carols, a free concert by the church, is hotly anticipated despite being weeks away.

INSIDE THE SANCTUARY, choir members lead the congregation in song. But the sight to behold is the organ, its pipes forming the singers' backdrop. The narrow steel pipes reach upward to the heavens, ringing out in celebration. The music itself is traditional, matching the tone set by a congregation comprised primarily of families and senior citizens. Reverend Carlson notes the significant portion of working professionals in the congregation, many of whom are researchers or professors at nearby Michigan State University.

The church has been steadily growing since its founding in 1964, when it had only 100 members. Prior to that, Reverend Howard Kedhe, the founding pastor, hosted worship services in his home. When services became overwhelmed with worshippers, the congregation moved to Okemos High School, then settled into its own building in 1968. Today, new members are typically recent arrivals in the community, newcomers to the Christian faith or people who are finding their way back to a church after periods of doubt, apathy or disillusionment.

A great deal of the church's past is visible in the current building, as the original chapel is still actively used. Small in comparison to the sanctuary, Kedhe Chapel—named for the church's first spiritual leader—now hosts events, adult education classes and self-help and support groups. Touring the classrooms, Reverend Carlson recalls the congregation's humble beginnings when Reverend Kedhe worked as a chemist during the week and led the congregation on weekends. The refurbished exterior is complemented by visible historical fixtures, cementing the importance of honoring and remembering past legacies while moving toward a better future.

Reverend Carlson's office is hidden near the back of the building, adjacent to the original chapel. Inside, books fill the shelves while antiques from around the United States reflect his travels. Prior to joining the Okemos parish in 1996, he preached at churches in Ohio and New Mexico. A Southwestern influence abounds with Spanish iconography, statues and paintings decorating the office. He points to one bookend designed as a

The Reverend Dr. Robert Carlson addresses the congregation.

miniature freestanding replica of his former church in New Mexico. Mounted on the wall behind his desk is a painting of the grand Norwegian cathedral where his grandmother was baptized. The towering structure, steeped in tradition, has stood for centuries.

Though Reverend Carlson wears traditional black robes during the service, he dresses casually for office hours. Some members call him Pastor Rob, others Dr. Carlson, but most simply call him Rob without any title. Such attire and monikers enable his congregation to see him as both a spiritual leader and a member of the community at large.

Over the course of a given week, Reverend Carlson and a small part-time staff occupy the office, which remains quiet during the day but active with events during evening hours. College degrees and seminary certificates share wall space with pictures of children and grandchildren, nearly all of whom reside in the Okemos area and watch him preach every Sunday. It was at the Princeton Theological Seminary in New Jersey where he met his wife, who was among the first women to study for a master's degree at the seminary. After they settled in Okemos, their children observed that it was the first time they felt part of a racial majority because their previous churches had been multicultural blends, with a heavily Latino population in New Mexico and a diverse congregation in Cincinnati.

Now, as Reverend Carlson delivers his weekly message, he says he's enormously pleased with the way everything has worked out and where God brought him. Looking to the future, he hopes the church will grow and expand its ability to touch the lives of community residents. Existing programs—such as the Global Institute of Lansing that helps immigrant children and their parents obtain high school diplomas—are exceptional causes that deserve more attention and assistance. Through volunteers, the program graduated nineteen participants last year and hopes to continue this success for years to come. Another activity likely to continue is the church's annual Crop Walk to raise money for local efforts to feed the hungry.

STANDING IN FRONT of his congregation, Reverend Carlson opens his Sunday message unconventionally, discussing the stages of grief as related through the recent television smash-hit series *Breaking Bad*. By chronicling the trials and tribulations faced by high school chemistry teacher Walter White as his life is transformed by methamphetamine, he explains the importance of accepting responsibility for one's actions. "Walter White illustrates a paradox that the apostle Paul writes about in Romans 7: 'When I want to do what is good, evil lies close at hand.' Human beings are creatures of mixed motives." In the same narrative, he fascinates the congregation with a tale of overcoming personal trials. Detailing the story of an internment camp during World War II, he talks about a prisoner who scraped the butter from his morning and afternoon bread and collected it

"The Good Shepherd" carved from driftwood welcomes worshippers as they enter the church.

in his pocket, much to the chagrin of his children. However, at the end of the week, after retrieving some hidden thread, he crafted a makeshift candle and burned it on days of worship. Reverend Carlson still finds this commitment inspiring.

Reverend Carlson prefaces each prayer with "from the rising of the sun to its setting," and worshippers respond, "Let the name of the Lord be praised." As the service concludes, he rushes to the entryway to shake hands and speak with the worshippers. After the service, congregants attend a wedding shower for members Laura Nieusma and her fiancé, Andy Welch, offering small gifts and encouragement. Though a few visitors leave immediately following the service, most linger on, enjoying one another's company.

19

A Passionate Few
— Quan Am Temple, Mason

By RJ Wolcott with photography by Katie Stiefel

TRAVELING DOWN COLLEGE ROAD, past the commotion of Michigan State University's campus, rolling green pastures become commonplace as the world simplifies into a reserved stillness. Eventually, emerald fields transition to craggy clumps of trees whose jagged branches extend to create an impenetrable wall along the cracked and winding roadway. It's here amid the woods that the Quan Am Temple stands solemnly outside Mason.

While images of pristine white shrines and crowds of robed holy figures often come to mind, Quan Am diverts from the stereotype of Buddhist temples. Members and spiritual seekers travel here from across Michigan in search of answers to life's most ponderous perplexities. And it is here, with two distinct groups of practitioners and a past worthy of retelling, where many find tranquility.

Newcomers can be forgiven for missing the temple, whose

Practitioners meditate

small red sign serves as its only visible roadside indicator. Turning into the complex, they see a lawn punctuated by a tall statue of Quan Am, from whom temple-goers take inspiration. Carving through the surrounding grounds is a subterranean network of streams. They rise to the surface in spots where adherents once released goldfish into the waters as a traditional sign of respect.

The one-lane blacktop road leads further into the complex that used to be a plumber's home and workshop but has been renovated to accommodate two live-in nuns and the temple itself. Additional statues reflecting Buddhism's past offer a sense of protection from the engulfing darkness while attendees' cars crowd the parking area. The temperature plummets as Anna Fisher welcomes guests, apologizing for the chilly climate in the converted tool shed. Hanging tools and heavy equipment occupied the interior that is now adorned with a colorful cascade of statues and writings. Oil spots and heavy machinery have been replaced with Vietnamese pottery and artifacts, instructional DVDs, literature and prerecorded lessons. Traditional Vietnamese music plays as practitioners make their way into the temple's meditation hall, an illuminated statue of the Buddha watching as they take seats on cushions placed neatly on the floor.

Meditation during a Thursday evening service

WITHIN THE SMALL community of English-speaking practitioners, which ranges from eight to fifteen attendees every Thursday, each has a story of how he or she found Buddhism.

For Fisher, the path to Quan Am came about as a result of community activism. In 2004, Fisher read a story in *The State News* about the existing local Buddhist temple losing its location in Lansing. Fisher felt compelled to help the group of mostly Vietnamese refugees who practiced there. And after meeting with the temple's monk and gauging his attitude, she knew she could offer to help. "He, without any resentment or any bad feelings, just said, 'Oh, it's okay, we'll move, it's okay,'" she says.

Soon the members of the Vietnamese community found and purchased the current rural site. But making friends with the neighbors proved an additional challenge, as offerings of candles and gifts failed to win hearts and minds. Fisher said, "People were very cold to us. It was just me and three Vietnamese, and I did most of the talking." Indeed, when Ingham Township held a hearing about a special use permit, "all the neighbors came out and they did not want a temple here. It was 2004 and I had never seen such an opposition in my life." The temple eventually won the required permit and set off to renovate the site.

Quan Am hosts not only members of the former Lansing temple but also a budding group of native-English speakers. Thursdays feature an English-language service and

Sunday services are conducted in Vietnamese, but the groups interact and meld through holiday services and the day-to-day upkeep of the temple.

These two groups—the more vocal, active English speakers and the more reserved immigrants—contribute to the spirit embedded within the temple. Two enormous tribute boards flanking the main hall's entrance feature photographs of deceased members from both groups and their families. The statue of Quan Am, the Bodhisattva of Compassion, exemplifies the dichotomy: One side features a retelling in Vietnamese of her significance, and the other side does the same in English.

Despite the gloomy weather, Fisher couldn't seem happier as she meanders through the grounds. Encircling the temple is a series of bricks donated by local and international supporters, and after some searching Fisher finds her name alongside her dog's on a brick near the edge of the display.

Raised in a traditional Catholic family, Fisher is still awed by how at peace she felt upon first entering a Buddhist temple. Talking now about Quan Am, Fisher feels that while it hasn't answered all of life's big questions, the temple's existence provides for the emotional and spiritual well-being of those within the community.

THE THURSDAY EVENING session at Quan Am is primarily a quiet time, as much of it revolves around meditation. Warm, low lights illuminate a room split into those sitting on cushions and those sitting on chairs. Meditation positions are varied, some determined, others relaxed. A few perplexed faces dot the group. The world around those present slowly closes in, the external becoming muted under the heft of internal thought, as they remove themselves from the physical world as much as possible. Some concentrate on breathing, some count, others keep their methods of meditation and prayer private.

Suddenly a member signals the end of sitting meditation by striking a large bell. As if they've rehearsed hundreds of times before, the group stands and bows, both to the Buddha and to one another. Then deliberately, the group walks mindfully, encircling the large meditation hall, practicing walking meditation. Members continue meditating as they shuffle or slowly walk. After a few passes, the group again bows and rearranges into a circle in the middle of the room. The circle itself symbolizes the group, as everyone involved is as much a part of the discussion as anyone else.

Conversations flow from readings that address the teachings of the Buddha. Perched on their pillows, members address the text as both a lesson and as an application to their daily lives. While some remain silent during the discussion, others muse aloud on the natures of being and energy and how suffering exists in the world. Some speak at length about meditation and the pursuit of *enlightenment,* a sense of knowledge of all things and

Depictions of the Buddha in front of the meditation room

the overwhelming peace that results. As the illuminated Buddha looks on, the practitioners wrap up their discussion and plan for future lessons revolving around Buddhist texts. After three final deep bows, the group slowly makes its way to the lobby.

A period of conversation and camaraderie takes place as members sit and talk around the great long table running through the temple's entry hall. Scattered on the table are documents and books for curious minds to ponder, some explaining the basic tenets of Buddhism and others detailing the dietary practices of many Buddhists. Guidance about worship and traditions is available on the temple's website.

Member Jean Morciglio says services never get too crowded for the temple, and Fisher admits that outreach has been difficult. While she would enjoy seeing more

Members sit in a circle to discuss Buddhist theology.

practitioners, resources are limited and the temple's comparatively remote location also poses a problem, especially with the small size of the Buddhist community in mid-Michigan. Still, members carry on with enthusiasm whether there are ten or 10,000 present.

Out of respect, worshippers had removed their shoes upon entering the temple, despite the cold floors, and they now reclaim their footwear as they prepare to head home. A Michigan State professor leans near the entryway, discussing classes and students, while others nearby speculate on the number of instructional tapes and CDs that clutter the glass display cases. Slowly but surely, members plunge into the cold October evening, passing the illuminated statuary as they depart.

Fisher seems content. Even without a flashy website or an on-site teacher, members still find harmony through the teachings of the Buddha and a sense of community and safety with those around them. As the temple lights flicker off and cars slowly work their way through the darkened compound, the statues and the temple itself remain, testaments to the strength and reliance of a community not of many but of a passionate few.

A statue of Avalokiteshvara, the god/goddess of compassion, stands in front of the temple. The figure is considered to be either male or female.

20

In the Light
— Red Cedar Friends, Lansing

By Jordan Jennings with photography by Elizabeth Izzo

A SQUARE ROOM speckled with multi-sized square, rectangular and diamond-shaped windows allows morning sunlight to cascade in on the expectant Friends. Rows of chairs face one another to create a square. About a dozen and a half people, mostly elderly, sit in silence. Thermoses of coffee rest at the feet of some. Many have their eyes closed, looking peaceful as if asleep. Some have furrowed brows like they're searching deeply within. Some look thoughtful, as if busy in conversation. A man in the corner straightens his neck upward and stares at something on the ceiling. A woman in a knitted blue cardigan sits unmoving and apparently content, hands in lap, eyes closed, gray hair pulled back in a ponytail, a faint smile on her lips.

After nearly ten minutes of silence, a man in a plaid flannel shirt and dress pants stands up and begins talking about a meeting he attended concerning investment in government and taxation. "Focusing on doing something useful rather than on making more money would have a profound effect on society." He pauses thoughtfully. Meanwhile, a housefly zooms in and out of the sunlight, careening around heads and chairs as he ends his verbalized thought and sits back down.

Silence descends on the room again.

The fly *flick-zap-skips* off one window. Occasionally an explosive cough sounds. Then one or two sneezes. Then a deep breath. Then the sound of fabric friction from a worshipper repositioning. The flicking leaves of the lilac bush outside make more movement than any members of Red Cedar Friends in the room this Sunday morning.

In contrast to the rushed lifestyle and atmosphere our modern culture demands, this gathering has an aura of unrushed timelessness. It's not the kind of timelessness that comes with wasting time sunbathing on a beach, napping or sitting in a doctor's waiting room. It is a timelessness that welcomes interaction with eternity, soul and self, rather than just mind and body.

FRIENDS TRY TO live according to the five Quaker testimonies: simplicity, peace, integrity, community and equality. A modern-day example is Meeting Clerk Carolyn Lejuste's choice to rarely use her microwave, a decision that helps her to maintain simplicity in her own life:

> If I can find ways in which I can prepare my food, cook it up slowly, appreciate it, I can often notice that the Spirit is working with me. Modern society is so fast and so complex that it takes us away from our sense of connection with the Divine.

Quakerism does not have a doctrine. Rather, adherents believe that God speaks to individuals directly. This allows Quaker belief to work in tandem with other faiths. Clerk Lejuste says that their Meeting attendees include those who are nontheist, Christocentric and Buddhist, among others.

A LATECOMER'S SHOES *click-clack-click-clack* on the faux hardwood floor as she enters.

Another woman stands. She is hesitant. "Vocal ministry is hard for me, as maybe it is for some of you." Then she uses a metaphor involving a rock and a ripe fruit to describe her temerity in sharing with the group. "Here I am, Lord," she says. "So I'm thinking that instead of waiting for the dynamite to blow me from my seat, I should be waiting for the small nudges." She seems humble, prodded in spirit to confront her temerity. She clears her throat periodically.

Silence. Expectancy. Timelessness. Another forty minutes of it.

"Are there those who would share a joy or sorrow or concern out of the spirit of this Meeting?" Clerk Lejuste asks firmly. She has black hair with icy spiked bangs. Red high-top

The Meeting of the Red Cedar Friends in silent worship

Converse shoes peek out from below her dark pants. She wears a plain, gray pinstriped button-up blouse and modest gold hoop earrings. No one here wears flamboyant attire.

Her full title—Clerk of the Red Cedar Monthly Meeting Religious Society of Friends—suggests that her position is one of religious authority. But because Red Cedar's Friends are unprogrammed Quakers, meaning they don't have clergy or a predetermined worship schedule, that's far from the case. Like all positions in the Meeting, Clerk Lejuste was nominated, and then the body of members approved that nomination. A nominating committee goes through *discernment* about who might be a good person to serve in a position, she explains. "Quakers are known for their process of consensus." A clerk's term lasts one year, and each clerk can serve only three terms.

Longtime Red Cedar Friend Richard Lee later describes his view of the clerk's role during their monthly Meeting for Healing:

The clerk draws up seven or eight requests, chooses the order, listens to God and, from the written list, is guided by the Spirit about which to put out first for prayer, how to frame each request and how long to spend on each request. The clerk's got a lot of responsibility, a lot of power. She's going to be guided by the Spirit. It's very mystical.

Lee joined Red Cedar Friends in October 1984 after starting to get active with Quakerism in 1966 with his grandparents in England. Lee says that he is a healer, psychic and teacher who leads workshops teaching Quakers about root beginnings, testimony and healing prayer.

Lee also leads a prayer group at his house. When his close friend Mario developed a dangerous case of gangrene, the group prayed for months. The disease, he explains, is "not readily curable. In this case, Mario got cured. The problem with that is that it wasn't normal, so they wouldn't let him be released from the hospital because they could be sued." After some uncertainty and a CT scan, the hospital staff finally released Mario. Even so, "a lot of Quakers don't believe in healing prayer anymore," Lee adds.

The Friends begin sharing prayer requests—or as they put it, asking "prayers to encircle them" and asking to be "held in the Light": "I ask Friends to hold [so-in-so] in the Light." "Please hold me in the Light."

This idea of holding one another "in the Light" draws from the perception of God, or the Spirit, as being the Light of truth, direction and wisdom. Rather than popcorn praying for one another—that is, hastily reciting prayers to make sure everything on their prayer list is checked off—the Friends simply hold the request before the Higher Being. They patiently let their prayers ascend before God.

Apart from the one-hour Meeting for Worship on Sundays, some Friends also gather for a half hour each weekday morning to "start their day off right." In addition to the four to eight who meet during the week, Clerk Lejuste and her partner Joann's dog, as well as another member's dog, also attend. The pets lay quietly during the Meeting.

RED CEDAR FRIENDS has existed for about fifty years. A decade ago, the congregation purchased land and put $50,000 worth of sweat equity into raising the building. A member with a portable sawmill processed the wood trim. Friends contributed much of the manual labor, including detailed tiling in the bathroom and the kitchen design specifications.

Because Quakers frequently call God *the Light*, the architect designed the windows so that sunlight illuminates the room. Clerk Lejuste says the building embodies "quiet elegance" and contains "nothing to take your attention away from going inside yourself and finding God."

Windows in the meetinghouse were designed to bring light in. They provide the only decoration in the room.

Meeting Clerk Carolyn Lejuste, Joann Neuroth and their dog Dalva worship on a Wednesday morning.

AFTER A BRIEF break for snacks in the hall area after Sunday worship, a handful of members reconvene in the room for their monthly Meeting for Business. Clerk Lejuste presents the first query, or question to be addressed, and there is a substantial pause as the group ponders it with characteristic silence for a few minutes. Why do the Friends respond to everything so slowly? That's because "divine Spirit is in that room. If we slow down during business and consider, leave space for everybody to speak, we will find a solution that is in unity with Spirit," Clerk Lejuste explains.

After each comment, a woman with blonde hair types notes. Her name is Kri Burkander. As the Recording Clerk, she assists the Meeting Clerk with documenting and overseeing the Meeting. Every Meeting of Business in more than 350 years of Quaker history has been documented somewhere, Clerk Lejuste says.

The group discusses plans for a new sign for the building. Lawncare and snow clearance for the upcoming winter are also mentioned before the group moves on to the weightier issue of their Eyes Wide Open exhibit. As soon as the topic of the exhibit is broached, an air of heavy emotion descends on the room. The exhibit is a way to demonstrate the tragic cost of human involvement in the Iraq War.

"Quakers are one of the traditional three peace churches," Clerk Lejuste explains. "We believe there is never a reason for war. The testimony is about peace. If there is 'that of God' in everybody, then we want to seek unity among everybody, not conflict. And we don't believe that conflict can be reasonably resolved through war." And Lee says, "We don't pray over the troops and then send them off to war to kill people, which a lot of churches do."

Eyes Wide Open displays a pair of combat boots for every member of the U.S.

military who has died in the wars in Iraq and Afghanistan. Each pair of boots is matched with the name and date of a soldier's death. The exhibit also includes civilian shoes, with each pair representing ten civilian Iraqis killed. Posters talk about the cost of war, and combat pictures show civilian victims.

With 3,000–4,000 names and pairs of combat boots alone, the national exhibit is too big to travel. Thirty-seven eighteen-gallon bins contain more than 150 shoes. While the Red Cedar Friends want to continue managing the Michigan exhibit, transportation has become difficult. Although it used to be a national project, only Friends in Indiana, Virginia and Michigan have exhibits left.

Courses of action are suggested. Ideas are contributed. Heads nod. Women weep as they discuss the generations lost in war. Clerk Lejuste explains why the discussion is emotional:

Many of us have brought that exhibit to places or have nurtured it. We know the names of those people. We have memorized their names and met their families. It is a very tender, tender project. In the end, you cannot walk away without a sense of the cost of war.

Teenager Teagan Grady's parents brought her to Red Cedar Friends as soon as she was born, and she's been coming her whole life. "As a young person, I feel like there's a lot more respect given to us than in other communities. Your opinion is taken into consideration like you can think intelligently. They would listen." She speaks confidently with an air of maturity and no evidence of teenage giddiness.

Another teen, Matt Shaw, sits next to her on the piano bench. Shaw's parents were involved with Red Cedar Friends, and when they adopted Matt at 9 months, they involved him too. "It exposed me to a lot of things. We're very pro-choice, pro-gay. It's taught me to be very open-minded, to be kind."

Although Shaw hated coming to Meeting when he was younger, both he and Grady agree that it's their personal choice to continue attending. "They're the coolest people—and probably the scariest—you'll ever meet," Grady says of the adult Friends, "They say things that normal people would not say. They're not afraid of being judged, so they'll just lay it out there, and it can be scary but intriguing."

Clerk Lejuste says that kids "are very much an equal part of our Meeting." At First Day, the Friends' Sunday morning children's classes, young children are read books about Quaker history, told stories from the Bible and told stories about understanding their own emotions.

Preteen youth learn meditative drawing techniques, such as Zentangles. They learn about historical social issues, which gives them an efficient way to quiet and calm themselves, Clerk Lejuste says. "One of the unique things that Quaker kids learn is quiet. We work generally with our children to find ways for them to go inside and do reflection."

21

Air of Change
— River Terrace Church, East Lansing

By RJ Wolcott with photography by Jordan Jennings

I N THE SHADOW of Hubbard Hall, Pastor Sam Perry gazes out his office window, meandering through the memories of youthful times spent at Michigan State University just across the street. Fall is heavy upon the active college community as cascading leaves tumble onto the few cars in the River Terrace Church parking lot.

Having grown up in Midland, Pastor Sam—as his congregants casually call him—remembers his path to the ministry as a personal challenge. In fact, the operative phrase in his eyes is "kicking and screaming." After years of outreach work, including missionary efforts in China, he finally embraced what his colleagues had been urging for years and embarked on a clerical path. Now, just over a year after arriving in East Lansing from his first congregation in Colorado, he finds River Terrace an exciting opportunity to return home. And while he commemorates his past adventures—most poignantly in the corner of his office where a feudal sword rests somberly within its sheath—his mission lies here. Anyone observing the pastor's office would be struck by its businesslike atmosphere. Stacks of papers line his desk alongside knickknacks and photos. Large oak bookshelves cover two walls, swelling with tomes ranging from spiritual lessons to bird-watching guides.

At the office table, he appears relaxed and collected, his dark-framed glasses resting just below a groomed mop of silver hair. While the church draws a substantial amount of its membership and energy from the nearby campus, he strives to keep authentic, applicable biblical concepts in the forefront. "We are definitely a university town and we could go the route of a purely academic faith, but we want to engage head and heart. That would be consistent with our vision of 'engaging hearts and minds to flourish in Christ.'"

Founded in 1934 by eleven Dutch members of the Christian Reformed Church, River Terrace's first building was constructed in 1947 several miles from its current location. After moving closer to campus in 1969 and building numerous additions in the late 1990s, the congregation has swelled to well over 500 members, according to Eunice Bossenbrook, who's worked for the church for more than thirty years.

Inside the long, narrow sanctuary with its globes of lights hanging from golden wires and television screens flanking either side of the pulpit, the pews are packed with parishioners. There's the old guard in suits standing in contrast to the young families often cradling newborns while trying to keep squirming toddlers in their seats. The congregation contains a vibrant tapestry of families, with children driving the church's many youth programs. When beckoned by Assistant Pastor Ken Bieber, a seemingly endless stream of children hops off the wooden pews, running—or, at the insistence of their parents, walking—toward the front. Afterward, they scurry to Sunday school to the tune of modern Christian hymns.

The children's lessons aren't the only reminder of the kinetic energy pulsing through the congregation. With more children come more baptisms, and it isn't uncommon to see multiple baptisms each week. A new baptismal font, adorned with a delicate glass bowl perched on wooden supports, stands in front of the lectern.

Sitting at his L-shaped wooden desk where bobblehead dolls of Protestant Reformation theologian John Calvin and television star Dwight K. Schrute of *The Office* share space with piles of paper, Pastor Sam explains how he understands what life can be like for parents with young children: He and his wife Sandee have five sons. They all attend church-related activities, but Pastor Sam says he's never felt pressured to blend his family life with his pastoral life. Rather than heading a large fellowship program or chairing the choir, his wife prefers a smaller role within the congregation.

Throughout worship services and within the core of the church lies a casual foundation. Pastor Sam prefers to forgo fancy clerical garb or robes and admits that even a suit

The sanctuary is lined with stained glass windows. This dove symbolizes the Holy Spirit.

and tie on Sunday feel a bit too formal. He preaches primarily with personal anecdotes and folksy metaphors to convey his spiritual message. Whether he's talking about long summer months puttering around on boats with his best friends or speaking about his family, congregants face forward attentively, taking in the lesson.

Walking through the empty sanctuary on a weekday, Pastor Sam explains that while modern innovations are present, including flat screen TVs, microphones and projectors, River Terrace reflects a dichotomy of styles. The late morning Sunday service includes modern hymns and technology, but during the 9 a.m. worship he turns all of it off, except the microphones, and incorporates more traditional music. During the later service, five singers and musical instruments, including an acoustic guitar and drum set, substitute for the choir of the earlier service.

While the first members were primarily of Dutch descent, Bossenbrook says the

Dutch are now only one of many groups attending River Terrace. And while the church is embedded with rich traditions and history, there's a noticeable air of change. For example, Bossenbrook, with her institutional memory of that history, is set to leave her position with Service Ministries—a loss Pastor Sam is still coming to terms with. The previous minister was in place for more than thirty years, and many congregants have belonged for a good portion of that time. The addition of modern technology in the worship hall was also unsettling for many longtime members, many of whom prefer lower-key music and picking up a hymnal rather than reading from a massive screen at the front of the sanctuary.

Yet Pastor Sam believes his church cannot ignore new equipment, especially when it enhances the service and creates a more comfortable environment for professionals and their families. "People are so used to technology in their daily lives that it seems strange to not have it, even within the church." He also hopes that one day Sunday attire will no longer be a concern and that the division in dress between the two services—the early formal and the later casual—will come into harmony.

THROUGHOUT THE WEEK, River Terrace engages a constant flow of volunteers working at desks, cooking meals, stacking chairs and moving to and fro through the nursery, kitchen, meeting areas, gymnasium, library and hang-out centers. Community groups often rent space for their own activities, helping fund River Terrace's widespread outreach, including parolee support, food distribution and campus programs.

During the October 13 service, for example, a second offertory plate weaves its way through the congregation in support of the River Terrace Church Prison Ministry, an extension of Pathway of Hope, which brings the message of God to inmates. Money raised through plate-passing helps recently released prisoners reintegrate into the community through employment assistance. Other Pathway of Hope programs operating under River Terrace's Faith-in-Action efforts include free Wednesday night dinners for area residents who are hungry for a hot meal and warm company.

However, the crown jewel of River Terrace's outreach efforts is Campus Edge, a program for MSU graduate students that the church started a few years before Pastor Sam's arrival. Students, faculty and staff blend their professional ambitions and careers with a connectivity to faith and service. Campus Edge's mission statement is "to provide a caring, Christian campus community where passions of faith, learning, career, fellowship and service come together and flourish."

In addition to Bible study, faith projects and volunteer work, Campus Edge runs intramural sports programs, activity nights such as bowling parties and adult-targeted outings such as the CEF Brew Tour, where members tour local breweries in search of refreshment. The group also hosts more traditional and holiday events, providing a youthful forum for young adults to learn more about the Word of God.

River Terrace is pursuing an effort to remain relevant in the twenty-first century while expanding beyond the notion that Sunday service attendance is enough. Pastor Sam believes that while attending worship is important, spreading the message of God's grace throughout the community takes precedence. Whether in the form of volunteer work, events or simply engaging with others one-on-one regarding faith, he wants people to form a loving relationship with their Lord and Savior rather than being concerned about what tie to wear to church or bickering about which denomination is closest to God.

Most of all, he heads a congregation dissatisfied with simply bringing the family to worship once a week. It isn't about the singing or about feeling guilty for skipping church. He says he is more concerned with dealing with daily happenings than speculating about the future of the church. While he does want to see the church expand and reach more people, he doesn't spend his time plotting out such a course by the hour. Instead, he trusts in his Lord to provide.

THE MID-MORNING SUN shines through the tall, narrow windows in the back of the worship hall as congregants take their seats. The large projection screen, which previously displayed the lyrics to the spiritual slave song "Wade in the Water," has gone blank. Pastor Sam stands before the worshippers and invites the families of Nathan James Mangiavellano and August Keeley Smidt to the pulpit. The two anxious young couples make their way to the front, tightly clutching their infants while the congregation looks on in approval. Some other parents in the pews look at their own children who were baptized at the same font not so long ago. Older members grow sentimental, recalling their children's and grandchildren's big days.

After a brief prayer, the two babes are brought to the font. The pastor stands before the parents, lowers his hand into the bowl and splashes the waters of the Lord on their children. As their gentle cooing echoes through the silent sanctuary, he baptizes them in the name of the Father and of the Son and of the Holy Spirit, welcoming both Nathan and August into the welcoming arms of Jesus Christ, their Lord.

22

All the Ends of the Earth

— St. Gerard Parish, Lansing

By Leah Benoit with photography by Dylan Sowle

FATHER JOHN KLEIN always had a feeling he'd somehow end up serving the Church. He grew up as one of eight children in a Roman Catholic family and his parents encouraged their children to pursue whatever professions they wished, as long as they kept God involved in their decisions and in their lives. It was in college when Father Klein truly began to sense a calling to priestly ministry, and he turned to trusted priests he knew for guidance. After completing seminary, he was confident he'd made the right choice to pursue full-time ministry in the Church.

Today Father Klein is the pastor at St. Gerard Parish. If you're looking for him, you'll find him Saturday evenings and Sunday mornings greeting parishioners as they arrive for Mass. While he welcomes parishioners at one particular weekend Mass, young children approach the entering congregants, handing out baby bottles as part of a fundraiser for a local charity. Ushers pass out bulletins as families leave the sanctuary.

Congregants make their way into St. Gerard Parish for an afternoon Mass.

The parish welcomes worshippers through a large entranceway with floor-to-ceiling windows that allow natural light to brighten the space. In the entranceway—which worshippers call the Gathering Area—just outside the sanctuary, a plaque commemorating Holy Cross Parish, the mother church of St. Gerard, adorns the wall. Upon entering the sanctuary, parishioners dip their fingers into the holy water that fills the baptismal pool, making the Sign of the Cross as they make their way to their seats.

St. Gerard is the spiritual home to more than 2,800 households, amounting to about 8,000 individual members. On a typical weekend about 3,200 worshippers attend Sunday Mass, including about 700 at the most popular service at 11 a.m.

ESTABLISHED IN 1958, St. Gerard initially served mostly blue-collar autoworkers and their young families on Lansing's Westside. Over the years, the makeup of the church membership has fluctuated due to changes in the auto industry. Yet, many of the original families remain. Today the parish, while still having many young families, has more senior citizens than ever as its charter members age. Members are predominantly white, while Hispanics make up about 5 percent of the parish population. Another 5 percent have their roots in India or the Philippines. The growing number of black parishioners includes those born in the United States and Africa.

On this Saturday evening, the pews are a little more than half filled and many worshippers are present with their families, which Father Klein stresses is of utmost importance to the Church. Attire is casual, and many parishioners are sporting Michigan State University apparel. There are seven sections of pews, angled to face a central altar, with a center aisle through which the opening procession moves. Altar servers lead the procession with candles, closely followed by a reader, a deacon with the Book of the Gospels and Father Klein as organ music leads the congregation in the entrance hymn.

A PARKING LOT separates the church from St. Gerard Catholic School, which serves 560 children in grades pre-K through eight. It was designated a School of Distinction in 2007 by the Michigan Association of Non-Public Schools and has long been a source of pride for the pastors and people of St. Gerard. Students follow a curriculum that integrates standard subjects with daily lessons of the Catholic faith. Children who don't attend St. Gerard School participate in weekly religious education classes designed to form them in the faith. Children in both the school and the religious education program are prepared to receive the Sacraments, including First Communion, Reconciliation and Confirmation.

Father Klein emphasizes the importance of allowing children to feel part of the Church from a young age. During Mass young children join their parents in reciting prayers, including the "Our Father."

> *Our Father, who art in heaven,*
> *hallowed be thy name;*
> *thy kingdom come;*
> *thy will be done on earth as it is in heaven.*

Give us this day our daily bread;
and forgive us our trespasses
as we forgive those who trespass against us;
and lead us not into temptation,
but deliver us from evil. Amen.

During Mass younger children entertain themselves with books and coloring while older ones follow along with adult worshippers, focusing on the message of the day.

The Scripture readings of the day, along with many prayers including the "Our Father," are the same in churches around the world. "The Catholic Church is more structured than many other branches of Christianity," Father Klein explains. "We have a common leader, Pope Francis, who was just elected this year. We have universal elements to our weekly worship including common readings every Sunday and a common structure to our worship."

Parishioners can anticipate and prepare the Scriptures that will be read at upcoming services and learn about parish events in a church bulletin distributed every week. Because of the structure and flow of the Mass, the hymns and prayers quickly become familiar, and even children can be heard joining in the refrain to Psalm 98:

All the ends of the earth have seen the power of God.

As Mass progresses past the Scripture readings and homily, parishioners bring the bread and wine forward to be prepared, blessed and consecrated at the altar. Catholics believe the bread and wine become the Body and Blood of Christ, commonly known as the Eucharist. After the prayers of consecration and blessing, Father Klein raises the Body and Blood of Christ and invites worshippers to come forward and participate in Holy Communion. Eucharistic ministers come forward from the congregation to assist him in the distribution of Holy Communion. As each parishioner steps forward, the host—the Body of Christ—is presented with the words, "The Body of Christ." The communicant responds, "Amen," indicating his or her belief that Christ is present. The host is received and placed on the tongue or in the palm of the hand. Those too young to receive Holy Communion are presented by their parents for a blessing. Some communicants move to a line where the Blood of Christ is sipped from the chalice. Having received Holy Communion, all return to their seats, where they kneel and offer prayers of thanks.

———————

Father Klein places high priority on knowing the names, needs and concerns of his parishioners, and he often studies the parish pictorial directory to learn their names. Though he takes seriously his role as a guide to his people in the ways of faith, he doesn't consider himself better than them, but rather a fellow pilgrim with those he leads. Though he may

Mass traditionally begins with a procession of younger members carrying a cross, followed by the pastor and associate pastor wearing robes.

be more studied in Scripture, theology and the life and traditions of the Church, he too must dedicate himself to following Christ even as he asks his people to do so. By being part of their lives, he tries to keep in touch with the challenges his people face. He attends most of the events and activities where his people are found. If he presides at a funeral, he goes to the luncheon that follows. If he officiates at a wedding, he goes to either the rehearsal dinner or the reception. If he's invited to a graduation party or anniversary celebration, he'll typically be there.

Father John Klein explains the history of the church.

FATHER KLEIN BELIEVES every parishioner has an integral role to play, and that the Church's mission won't succeed without them fulfilling those roles. "We want everybody to be aware that each of us shares the responsibility of bringing others to Christ. The task belongs to everyone, not just to the priests."

As part of the commitment to bringing the ministry of Christ to others, St. Gerard Parish and its school engage in outreach programs throughout the Lansing area. For example, they sponsor a tutoring and mentoring program in the Waverly school district.

The parish has an active St. Vincent de Paul Society that assists the poor. Every Wednesday evening its volunteers visit twenty-five to thirty homes of people in need, delivering food and personal items donated by parishioners. Once a year the parish takes on a building project working with Habitat for Humanity or the city of Lansing to provide a home for a family in need. In addition, St. Gerard actively supports a medical clinic in Nicaragua that assists women experiencing difficult pregnancies. This ministry has particular meaning for the parishioners since their patron, St. Gerard Majella, is the patron saint of pregnant women.

To encourage parishioners to reach out to others in need, Father Klein and the pastoral staff believe in the importance of treating all members with respect. As they grow in their own appreciation of their value and dignity in God's eyes, they become more highly motivated to affirm the value and dignity of those they seek to serve.

St. Gerard Parish works hard to provide and maintain the facilities necessary for its ministries to thrive. In addition to the sanctuary and school, the parish has meeting rooms, a social hall and offices for its pastoral staff. Parishioners can meet with pastoral staff to discuss issues of personal faith and life struggles such as divorce. Parishioners also come for help with preparing for marriage, baptism and other sacraments. In the front office, parishioners arrange for funerals and other services. The parish also schedules opportunities for the Sacrament of Reconciliation and other worship events.

While Father Klein remarks that there's nothing strikingly different about St. Gerard's message and structure than that of other local Catholic churches, there is a strong sense of community that keeps congregants enthused, engaged and willing to return. "All of this," Father Klein says of its ministries, services and activities, "is to communicate to the faithful that they are worth it—to me, to St. Gerard Parish and, most importantly, to God."

23

Dancing with God
— Sycamore Creek Church, Lansing

By Marisa Hamel with photography by Erin Hampton

M IKA ROTMAN USED to be a Mormon. "I was trying to find a turn of my own and branch out of my parents' church," she says. In doing so, she met her pastor-to-be, Tom Arthur, through a youth magazine's article about family. "I had sent him an email to get together to meet with him and he invited me to church."

At the time she started coming to Sycamore Creek Church, the daughter congregation of Holt United Methodist Church, Rotman and her mother had been estranged for years. She soon felt comfortable enough to invite her mother, Marian Wilson, to church with her, and within a few months Wilson joined the five-member band as a keyboardist playing on Sundays. Now, the family calls this their niche. Rotman gets a ride from other members on Sundays and helps in the nursery during the service. With a busy schedule working and caring for her infant child, she and her husband grab dinner and their weekly spiritual bread at

This setup illustrates the creative topic of Pastor Tom Arthur's series "Dancing with God."

Church in a Diner on Mondays at Jackie's Diner in Lansing. Rotman's husband likes the church's modern spin on religious lessons, including concepts like "dancing with God" or being "off the tracks" with faith. Soon there will be a four-week series called "Strapped" giving advice on becoming financially stable, something the couple could benefit from with a new addition to the family.

THE SERVICE CONCLUDES with an announcement. "Come alive on God's great dance floor!" Pastor Tom yells over the clanking of folding chairs being cleared from the lunchroom floor of Lansing Christian School. Swing dancing lessons are about to start, the big band has just arrived and the singer belts out a verse of "New York, New York" while the brass instruments tune up.

A Michigan State University Swing Dance Club teacher leads the congregation in dance.

Pastor Tom, as he prefers to be called, and his wife, Sarah Arthur, began dancing lessons after they got married and wanted to bring that energy to the church. Later, in one Monday night Church in a Diner sermon, he confesses that he loved the way his wife looked when an experienced dancer led her around the floor. It's similar to a relationship with God, a beautiful thing when the Master shows you the steps and you can say, "Aha! I got it!" and life makes sense.

You might wonder what a plate of omelets and toast, accompanied by YouTube videos, have in common with a United Methodist church. For Pastor Tom, they are alternative avenues to reach people's brains and plug them into God. He jokes that he spends too much time on YouTube finding clips that add a twist to his Church in a Diner sermons.

Most of the congregation consists of baby boomers and their families. Kids actively

Congregants join with members of the Michigan State University Swing Dance Club.

participate in the service by singing and dancing, and there are groups for children (such as Kids Creek) and teens (such as StuREV) coordinated by Sarah Arthur with the help of other congregants. With his mix, the Arthurs were instrumental in evolving Sycamore Creek's basic music and lessons into dynamic and original experiences, drawing connections between faith and daily life. The four-week series of sermons about dancing with God is an example of learning to dance with one another.

Pastor Tom says it's important "not to have traditionalism but keep tradition alive." Just as religion is tied to tradition, so too is dance. Dating back to the 1920s, jazz-infused swing dancing—including its most popular version, the Lindy Hop—evolved from ballroom dancing. Some people resisted but it brought community and energy to the youth of the 1920s through 1950s. "What's so bad about that?" he wonders aloud during his sermon at the diner. In a reference to the book of Ecclesiastes, he talks about learning with others, "By yourself you are unprotected but with a friend you can face the worst," says Ecclesiastes 4:12, meaning in more contemporary language that it's "better to have a partner than to go it alone," just like it is hard to learn how to swing dance by yourself. How about a whole diner's worth of friends?" Pastor Tom asks.

His message is that people learn best to dance in a community of dance, and they learn the life of faith, to seek God, to love God best in a community of people who are trying to do it together. You don't always get the steps right—he's seen some people try for forty-five minutes and still step on their partners' toes during lessons—but at least they were present, at least they learned one step. Thus church is a dance floor with wallflowers, dancers with two left feet and expert Lindy Hoppers.

He closes the sermon with one question: "Can we be on that dance floor at Jackie's Diner?"

THE PURPOSE OF Church in a Diner is to attract people who are uncomfortable in a traditional church setting. In fact, Sycamore Creek doesn't own a space. Rather, it rents the school on Sundays, and Jackie's Diner is open exclusively for its services on Monday night.

"The church isn't a building—it's the people in the building," Pastor Tom explains. "We can be a church in a diner, we can be a church in a bowling alley, we can be a church in a pub, because you, the people, bring God's presence with you."

Support groups, like Sycamore Creek's prayerful "pow-wows," are held by a dozen members in a circle between booths at the diner. Their heads bow together as if they're shooting prayers to the person across from them. The leader, a short and enthusiastic woman, asks what moved them during the service or whom they feel they should contact during the week. Prayers conclude and an announcement is made that other United Methodist churches in the area also started similar Church in a Diner programs. They cheer—their quirky congregation seems to be catching fire.

"We're not the dead faith of the living," says Pastor Tom. "Bring your questions: The more you learn about God, the more questions you have about who He is." Congregants "are human, and they improve with each plate of eggs and each swing-dance lesson." As he tells the congregation, "Sunday morning is the practice and the rest of the week is the game." It doesn't matter which church you are a part of or which dance you are comfortable with—ballroom, hand jive, boogie-woogie or rock and roll—but it's important that you dance.

Pastor Tom is proud of his congregation's attitude toward life and commitment to God, themselves and others. "The church isn't always at its best, but when it is, I think this is what it looks like."

24

Where There Is a Need, We Are Here to Help
— Trinity African Methodist Episcopal Church, Lansing

By Leah Benoit with photography by Ashley Weigel

IT'S QUITE EARLY to be up and about, particularly on a Sunday. The parking lot at Trinity African Methodist Episcopal Church is nearly empty. Sunlight is barely creeping in through the stained glass windows along the right side of the building, casting a soft glow amongst the nearly empty pews. Red carpeting covers the floor of the sanctuary, complementing the red decorations that surround the altar up front. A single aisle separates the two seating sections, while a large illuminated cross hangs on a brick wall behind the altar. Outside, the sun is beginning to rise above the large white wooden cross attached to the roof.

And yet the ushers are alert and ready to greet the handful of worshippers who've arrived for the 7:30 a.m. abbreviated service. Of the dozen or so gathered, nearly all are over the age of 50.

For Pastor Lila Martin, all are familiar faces. She stops to speak with each congregant individually, asking about things

Worshippers pray at the front of the sanctuary.

going on in their lives. To an outsider, she appears to be a friend as much as a pastor.

"Our members are fairly consistent," she says over coffee and doughnuts after the service. "We see the same people week after week. They like coming here." She tries to get to know all of them on a personal level, something she finds critical, not optional. "As a pastor, I expect them to be faithful and be loyal, and by the same token I will be faithful, loyal, love them and take care of them. How can I do that if I don't know who they are?"

FOUNDED IN 1866, Trinity African Methodist Episcopal Church is the spiritual home to almost 400 members, most of them African American, although some congregants are biracial or Hispanic. Most are retirees. For many, Trinity has been their church for many years, and its oldest member is more than 105.

Trinity African Methodist Episcopal Church isn't Pastor Martin's first pulpit. A North Carolina native, she began her career in ministry at Garrett-Evangelical Theological Seminary in Evanston, Illinois. Having grown up in the faith, she served as an assistant

Pastor Lila Martin lifts donations to the cross.

pastor at St. Stephen AME Church in Detroit and pastored four AME churches before moving to Trinity in September 2011. She has been head pastor now for two years, and as a middle-aged African American woman, she's a peer to many of her congregants. Women slightly outnumber men at the church, and many of its worship services celebrate women and strong female characters throughout biblical history.

Fittingly, today Trinity celebrates Women's Day. Congregants and visitors participate in a special service and, upon arrival, receive pink breast-cancer ribbons to wear. Both morning services feature guest speaker Dr. Eva L. Evans, whose long history with Trinity has seen her serve as a trustee, a chair of Women's Day and a class leader. The message of the day centers on the heroine of the Old Testament book of Esther and whose story Evans intertwines with her own message of strength and faith.

Although she welcomes people of all ages and races, Pastor Martin suggests that the name and history of the denomination explain why a majority of members are African American. "Our name was chosen because we were formed over 200 years ago, and people of slavery and of African descent were seeking a place to worship freely. The name may give the impression that we are exclusively for people of color, but that's not the case."

Methodists acknowledge the existence of the Trinity—Father, Son and Holy Spirit—from which the church derives its name. The core message is that Jesus Christ died to save humanity from sin, and the emphasis is on giving and compassion.

Trinity regularly hosts events to encourage members to bring someone new and to

Worshippers pray together.

encourage individuals seeking a change in their lives to hear the church's message. For example, each January Trinity hosts Operation Andrew, with a focus on de-emphasizing the need to dress up for church. Each week of the month, the Sunday service has a different theme of dress, including sweats, bright colors, sorority or fraternity apparel and old-fashioned clothing. Pastor Martin says, "The most common excuse we hear for someone not coming to church is 'I have nothing to wear.' If we're all wearing casual attire, you have no excuse. We want people to understand that it's about what's in the heart, not appearance."

During services, visitors are invited to introduce themselves and explain what led them to Trinity. Newcomers may initially feel like they're on the spot, but current members then greet them, introduce themselves and thank them for joining them in worship. Late in the service, worshippers come together for a Moment of Power. The dozen or so congregants in attendance are scattered throughout the sanctuary, but on Pastor Martin's cue they rise and gather with those sitting nearest to them, joining hands and uniting to sing a hymn.

It's easy, in this way, to see where the sense of community that Pastor Martin speaks so highly of begins.

Although she hopes to see Trinity expand its numbers over the next few years, spiritual growth is more significant. "If there is any growth that is going to take place, you have to grow spiritually. Growth is more about understanding the message than just showing up every Sunday."

For members, part of spiritual growth comes from engagement in worship. While

Pastor Martin preaches, members spontaneously interject their agreement through calls of "Amen!" Their voices unite in song throughout the service. At the more widely attended 11 a.m. service, multiple choirs, dancers and speakers contribute to the message of the day.

A sense of unity emerges early in the service. Pastor Martin begins with a Call to Worship, to which congregants respond:

> *Let the words of my mouth and the meditation of my heart be acceptable in your sight, O Lord, my rock and my Redeemer.*

LATER, CONGREGANTS FILE to the front of the church for the Altar Call. There, they, along with Pastor Martin, surround the three-sided entrance to the altar and kneel in prayer. Though the early service offers enough room for all members in attendance to participate at once, there is frequently a line at the fuller 11 a.m. service so each worshipper may have a turn. The idea is to publicly reaffirm their commitment to God.

Before the service commences, Pastor Martin gives the floor to two members who take a moment to recognize several congregants for their faith. Names nominated by fellow congregants are called and applauded as Women of Faith, and Men and Women of Loyalty, Leadership, Courage, Beauty and Obedience. Those present are invited to the front of the chapel to accept a rose, a gift for exemplifying the attributes of Esther, whom the church holds in high regard.

Engagement is key for Trinity. Pastor Martin recalls a successful event last year, when members donated furniture and lightly used clothing to a free flea market open to Lansing residents. Trinity reached out to other churches to promote the event and participation. The results went well beyond expectations. "We opened at 9 a.m., and by 11 everything was gone. It really demonstrated to us that there is a need, and we can help fill it," she says.

Although external engagement is essential, supporting its own members is of even higher importance. Through an outreach and welfare program, members can apply for assistance with food, rent, clothing and bills. Funds are raised through donations. "This is a very giving community. Where there is a need, we are here to help."

Such support and the subsequent sense of community aren't limited to days of formal worship. The church hosts exercise classes on Monday and Thursday evenings. Sunday school is available for all ages, along with Bible study and daily prayer sessions. Pastor Martin believes an assortment of activities allows members to get to know one another and allows her to learn more about them.

A strong sense of community keeps members loyal to Trinity. And as the last members of the morning's first service trickle out of the church, she takes her place by the door, ready to greet early arrivals for the second service.

25

We've Got *an* Answer

— Unitarian Universalist Church of Greater Lansing, East Lansing

By Joshua Anderson with photography by Brittany Holmes and Jordan Jennings

I T'S THE APPRENTICE minister's first sermon at the Unitarian Universalist Church of Greater Lansing. Reverend Kathryn A. Bert, the usual face before the congregation every Sunday, is gone this week, leaving preaching duty to seminarian Julica Hermann.

Before Hermann begins, the congregation gathers in what's known as the Fireplace Room, although it's technically the same room as the sanctuary, which is known as the Assembly Hall. The two halves are divided only by a change in flooring: As soon as the carpet of the Assembly Hall gives way to the tile of the Fireplace Room, worshippers know they've crossed into the other side.

In the Fireplace Room, a number of information booths are set up with pamphlets laid out for the taking. "Meet the Unitarian Universalists," one reads, offering a nineteen-page summary of what the church believes. Another is snappier: "To the Point: 15 Unitarian Universalist Elevator Speeches."

Julica Hermann,
Apprentice Minister, and
Revered Kevin Tarsa,
Interim Minister of Music

"Welcome," reads the headline of a leaflet about the Unitarian Universalist church in East Lansing, although chances are that a newcomer couldn't approach an information table and read that word without first hearing it spoken by a greeter. Members are eager to shake hands and talk about what their congregation offers. After learning about its assortment of classes, fundraisers and events, it's not uncommon to begin a friendly conversation about what brought you here or how you learned about the faith. Between the unavoidable introductions, shy newcomers walk to the beverage counter. A tiny basket sits alone, asking for a small donation from the coffee drinkers.

As the service begins, the Fireplace Room empties and seats in the sanctuary fill. Soft blue walls covered with bright, handmade artwork keep the sanctuary distinct from the Fireplace Room. In the past there was a wall between the two sections, as there had been many other walls in the building as well. Before the church purchased the property in 1972, it had been a Jewish fraternity house. Back in the days of the giant dividing wall, the pastor had to stand in the doorway between the two rooms, one foot in each, and preach simultaneously to both sides.

At one time, there was a wall between the Unitarians and the Universalists as well. The Universalist Church arrived in Lansing in 1848, followed by the Unitarians, who formed a fellowship in 1948. By 1959 the two churches had merged locally, two years ahead of the national consolidation. It seems this church has a history of breaking down barriers.

THE SERVICE BEGINS with two songs, after which Hermann appears on the small pulpit at the front of the sanctuary and delivers the call to worship. She lights a chalice similar to the one depicted in the bright stained glass sign outside the entrance to the church. The flame is small but visible. Then, after greetings, singing and introductions, she takes the pulpit again, ready to dive into the week's message.

"Dumpy La Rue wanted to dance," she begins, addressing the congregation. "'Pigs don't dance,' said his mother. 'They bellow, they swallow, they learn how to wallow.'"

No, Dumpy La Rue isn't a divine object of worship for Unitarian Universalists, and no, Hermann hasn't gone crazy from stage fright. She's reading from *Dumpy La Rue*, a children's book, and the illustrations and rhyming prose are projected on a large screen in front of the congregation. Children are in the sanctuary, but most of the giggles and soundings of "aww" come from the adults.

After the apprentice minister reaches the final page of *Dumpy La Rue*, the children get up from their seats and are led to their youth classes to learn about the same topic as the adults, though the teachings are tailored to their age, of course. The congregation joins together in song once again, after which the minister begins her sermon, "Death and Rebirth." It's a difficult topic for children, the church's weekly pamphlet admits, but one in which they'll learn "that it's okay to ask questions."

Every week, fifteen minutes of the service are devoted to a "moment for all ages." It's not always a story, but the church fills the time with something that unites the children and adults all at once. "Church is one of the last remaining institutions where people of all ages get to mix," explains Reverend Bert, the senior minister. Preserving that bonding time is an important part of the weekly worship, and several times a year, the services are completely multigenerational.

As Hermann delivers her first sermon, she avoids specifics. "Death and Rebirth" is a topic that almost everyone has questions about, but solutions to age-old inquiries such as "Is there life after death?" and "What happens after we die?" are avoided.

If one were to ask Reverend Bert such a question face-to-face, she would respond by wondering why that's on your mind at the moment. Never, she says, would she stand before the congregation and proclaim the "correct" answers to tough questions like those. "The most I would say is, 'This is what I found to be true, for me.' There is no expectation that we would all believe the same thing." It's not as if she has the answer. Instead she would say, "We've got *an* answer."

The Unitarian Universalist church bills itself as a liberal congregation that embraces a multitude of beliefs and perspectives. "In our faith, God is not a given," explains one pamphlet from the Fireplace Room. "God is a question. God is not defined for us. God is defined by us." Reverend Bert likes to say that she has a "sense of humor about absolutes." As a result, her sermons focus less on faith and more on action. "One of the things that makes someone a Unitarian Universalist is a focus on this life and a desire to make this world better," she observes. "There's less interest in what happens after we die because that's all speculative." Christians, Jews, Hindus, atheists and all other types of believers and skeptics attend the church, united in their covenant to support each other.

Stained glass in front of Unitarian Universalist Church of Greater Lansing

FROM THE OUTSIDE, it's easy to assume that Unitarian Universalism has no commitments or requirements, but Reverend Bert insists that it's not as casual as it may seem. Rather, it's actually a challenge to have a church where diversity of belief is the expected norm. "The point of religious community is not to leave people out on their own, but ask, 'Where does your story connect with my story? What do we have in common?'"

While spiritual matters may be up for debate, most members find common ground when dealing with societal issues that the world faces today. Lately, for example, the church has partnered with another local congregation, St. Stephen's Community Church, to work toward ending mass incarceration, especially of African Americans. The week's handout reminds congregants that the Unitarian Universalists will have a presence at the Greater Lansing CROP Hunger Walk later that day. An environmental justice team will meet next week at 12:30 p.m. A showing of a film called *Trigger: The Ripple Effect of Gun Violence* will be followed by a discussion on the twentieth.

The church also reaches out to nearby Michigan State University, and this year is its first with a thriving campus ministry. With its liberal beliefs and non-dogmatic approach to answering theological questions, Unitarian Universalism seems like a logical fit for many college students. The campus is close by, but alas, just far enough away that it's easy to see how some students might prefer to sleep in on Sundays instead of attending services. Thus the church, says Reverend Bert, draws more professors than students.

Young adulthood is a time when many take a critical look at the religion of their upbringing, questioning the faith of their parents. Reverend Bert remembers her own path: born into Unitarian Universalism, visiting a "very conservative" Jewish synagogue in high school, then migrating to a "very liberal" one and eventually ending back where she started—the Unitarian Universalist church. In fact, her parents raised her in that faith to begin with because her father had learned about it in a world religions course. After having children, her parents wanted a church in which to raise them. They eventually moved to Utah, a place where it's "hard to be a part of the social atmosphere without having a church you can claim." The Unitarian Universalist church became very important to her family at that time.

IF REVEREND BERT had to pick a new location for the church, proximity to the university would be irrelevant. As the only Unitarian Universalist congregation in the Lansing area, many members will always have a bit of a travel each Sunday morning no matter where the building is located.

What to do with the current building is a big question on the congregation's mind. The church strives to make its facilities as physically accessible as possible, but there's room for improvement. The upper stories, where youth education takes place, aren't wheelchair-accessible, and the church currently has two children who need that accommodation. Reverend Bert says the church tries to make up for such shortcomings in other ways. During the 11:15 a.m. service on Sunday, for example, a team of American Sign Language interpreters take turns standing by the pulpit to interpret the spoken message for any deaf worshippers—even if no hearing-impaired members are known to be present that day. It can't hurt to be prepared.

While other churches are in the midst of confronting a "mass exodus"—scores of people, especially younger generations, leaving organized religion and emptying the Sunday-morning pews—Reverend Bert feels that, in a way, the Unitarian Universalist church has the opposite dilemma. "We're too big for our building," she says. The reason it can't grow is because it's already too full of congregants. As far as problems go, there are certainly worse ones to have.

HERMANN CONCLUDES HER first sermon by extinguishing the flickering chalice. Everyone in the congregation stands and speaks the affirmation aloud in unison:

With faith in love,
we are building community,
growing and changing together. Peace.

185

26

Called to Give Drink to the Thirsty

— University Lutheran Church, East Lansing

By Jordan Jennings with photography by Olivia Hill

T HE METALLIC OVERTONES and pale undertones of a nine-teenth-century organ reverberate through the sanctuary. An organist plays reverently, her voice joining those of the sparse congregation. Pastor Fred Fritz's voice is a rich vibrato-filled baritone.

An abstract slanted ceiling slopes toward the rainbow stained glass windows that rise to meet it on both sides. The windows are the colors of a Rubik's Cube and douse the pews in Funfetti morning light. During the eighth and ninth centuries, stained glass was both a teaching device to tell biblical stories and a work of art, Pastor Fritz notes. With the invention of the printing press, they lost some of their instructional purpose and are currently used primarily for effect and mood.

Practice tables for the handbell choir and two grand pianos suggest music is an integral part of University Lutheran Church's Sunday worship service. A baptismal font and candle wait at the

Pastor Fred Fritz sings from the Gospel at the close of worship.

entrance to the sanctuary. You can draw a water cross on your forehead before worship, or afterward before going into the world, Pastor Fritz explains, "Whatever's helpful for your faith walk."

Apart from the Michigan State University students who mostly attend the second Sunday service, the congregation generally consists of MSU professionals and faculty and their families, state employees and other well-educated adults. Even if the members don't attend or work at the university, they typically have season football or basketball tickets or attend Wharton Center events.

That's to be expected since University Lutheran began as a student group on campus. Organized in 1941, the congregation met in the Old State Theatre for seven years. During the 1940s and 1950s, congregants built a church that the Seventh-day Adventists now use. The current building, on South Harrison Road across from campus, was built in 1971.

"Do you like surprises? Sometimes they can be scary because you don't know what's going to happen, right?" Pastor Sara Cogsil sits on the carpeted steps and speaks gently to a child during the kids' portion of the service. She wears white robes and a silver necklace-like pendant. Her voice is confident and clear with the warmth of a children's storyteller but the authority of a leader. She tells the story of Jacob wrestling with God from Genesis 32.

"Have you ever been surprised by God? God's a wrestler. Sometimes we are left blessed but limping."

Now she addresses the whole congregation: "Are we open to encountering God?

How many of us woke up this morning expecting to meet with God?" Her voice alternates between ending on a higher note and a lower note, creating a melodic, verbal pulse, a sway. "But it is here we can see God in the people we encounter. It is here we hear God in His Word. It is here we experience forgiveness through Holy Communion."

Pastor Cogsil is a lesbian, and not the only non-heterosexual clergy at University Lutheran. New intern Asher O'Callaghan, who greets the congregation with a combination of welcoming informality and solemn formality, is transgendered. O'Callaghan has one year of classes left at Luther Seminary in St. Paul, Minnesota. One reason he chose University Lutheran is because of its welcome statement's stance toward gender:

> In particular they include sexual orientation in that. That was really influential to me because I didn't want to end up at a congregation where I didn't feel like I could be out. I knew in interviewing that it was a place where it wouldn't be as much of an issue. And I interviewed with [people] who specifically told me that it won't be okay for you to be out.

While O'Callaghan's strong Lutheran beliefs and equally strong openness about sexual orientation seem to contradict each other, they actually go hand-in-hand. He attributes his Lutheran beliefs to a church service in Denver a few years ago. Prior to that, he hadn't heard of Lutheranism.

Many services later, O'Callaghan, who was born Mary, felt a calling. "I came out as bisexual in college. Kind of got alienated from the campus ministry I had been a part of and kind of left church for a few years. I was surprised that I found myself at a church I could stomach, who accepted the LGBTQ community." The Denver church conducted a re-naming rite during a service and introduced him as Asher before the Passing of the Peace.

Upon O'Callaghan's arrival at University Lutheran in July 2013, Pastor Fritz mentioned to the congregation that the new intern is transgender. O'Callaghan says, "It's not like people are like, 'Yay, you're transgender.' It's more like it's not an issue for people; it's not something they dwell on. It's not a hurdle in interacting with them or how they view me."

O'Callaghan teaches confirmation and high school classes. Once a month, on Sunday mornings, he preaches and leads evening worship at Burcham Hills Retirement Community. He also visits some of the church's forty members who are 80 years or older, many of whom are homebound or hospitalized. He sees those visits as an expression of the community of Christ.

GLOBAL CONSCIOUSNESS IS another defining characteristic of University Lutheran. A tour of the church reveals how deeply its local and global contributions run. With 780 members, it's a powerhouse of community involvement. Each room portrays a facet of that involvement and passion.

To begin, Pastor Fritz's office sets a tone of modern pastoral duties and attitudes. His desk is covered with papers, articles and a desktop PC. A colossal mosaic of shelved literature and theological tomes lines one wall. Grim reminders of Christ's death decorate other wall space: a pen drawing of Christ's crucifixion surrounded by mourners, a collage of gold and wooden crosses, a heavily crosshatched black-and-white print of Martin Luther holding a Bible and glowering coldly. At mention of the Luther print, Pastor Fritz explains mischievously, "I kind of keep him because the students think he's creepy—when you walk into the room, his eyes follow you."

The pastor's miniature Australian shepherd, Frodo, follows him calmly out of the office, carrying a metal paper clip between his front teeth. The dog habitually straightens paper clips with his teeth, never swallowing them.

Meetings for outside groups such as FAN (Families Against Narcotics) take place here, as well as English as a Second Language classes. Even as Pastor Fritz speaks, two Japanese women sit at the other side of the room with their English teacher, talking softly.

In the hallway, a chattering trail of six Hispanic children follows a Caucasian man. The man points to an object, saying a couple of words slowly and clearly. The children, undocumented immigrants hoping to reunite with their families, discuss it eagerly among themselves in Spanish before repeating the word in English. University Lutheran holds daily classes from 8:30 a.m. to 3:30 p.m., during which they learn math, social science and, most importantly, English. Vacation Bible School is another example of the church's global focus because 75 percent of the participants are international, Pastor Fritz says. Translators are needed for seven to eight languages, including Swahili, Chinese and Russian.

Along one wall of the hall are Rubbermaid totes and boxes of items, from printer cartridges and health kits to clothes and toiletries. The church participates in Food Movers, a food bank, every fourth Thursday of the month. When the program began, there were three recipient families. Now that number has grown to around eighty-four.

Pastor Fritz enthusiastically lists the wide-ranging community programs University Lutheran participates in. The church supports ten local agencies, including Ele's Place and the MSU Crisis Center, builds a Habitat for Humanity house each year, provides "blitz makeovers" for the home of a low-income seniors, hosts twelve-step groups such as Alcoholics Anonymous and Narcotics Anonymous and provides Christmas gifts to 200 needy recipients each year. "Do you interact with the broader community? What are your motives?" he asks rhetorically. "We just feel that we're supposed to be engaged in community because we're supposed to. Not to get more members."

The church also installed a furnace in Latvia and plans to drill a well in Tanzania with help from MSU's Engineers Without Borders. The well-drilling effort is of particular interest to the congregation. As he enters the church's main welcome area, Pastor Fritz points

Organist Beth Weidenaar and Pastor Fred Fritz harmonize.

overhead. Near the skylight is a statement painted in aqua: "We Are Called to Give Drink to the Thirsty."

"Do you know where your bottled water comes from?" he asks. "We can't solve all of the problems of the world but we can think about how we contribute to them."

No one may know this better than church member Tula Ngasala. A wife and mother of three, Ngasala and her children came from Tanzania to Michigan five years ago to join her husband, an MSU student. "We are Lutherans back home, so when we came here we were looking for a church close to where we live. When we came here, we did not have a car so we used to walk to church, which was very convenient. It just happened that it was the perfect thing for us."

Ngasala's parents live in Mabibo, a small community in Dar es Salaam, Tanzania, and struggle with the poor water conditions there. The main source is rainfall, and some people go around with a "big cart with big wheels" to sell water to neighbors. The water still must be boiled for safety.

"In Tanzania, they had the plan of drilling a well. They have been trying to raise money for a long time. But there are lots of things going on. They put it off until they had enough money." With two degrees in water quality, Ngasala's passion for solving the problem in her hometown is evident. She described the situation to the church, proposing it help fund a rainwater collection system and well. The church agreed, providing $2,000 from its endowment fund, which covered almost the entire cost of the project.

Through a retired civil engineering professor, the church connected with Engineers Without Borders. That group took over the project, going to Tanzania on an assessment trip. A team of undergrad students and mentoring professors are working on a well design. This coming summer, they anticipate returning to install the well.

Prayer quilting is another ministry the church prides itself on. Ngasala's volunteer group spent months making seventeen quilts. As Pastor Fritz explains, each is unique. In a room of the church resembling a corner of Jo-Ann Fabrics, members sew patterned quilts. Loose strings are left on each section. The prayer quilts are then laid out with a description of a person or situation, and those who walk by can pray and tie a knot. After all the knots are tied, the quilt is sent to the person who was prayed for. Over the past decade, members have sewn 1,300 prayer quilts, some of them for veterans and some for people in Tanzania. And some recipients ask that their quilts be buried with them in their caskets.

To CONCLUDE THE tour, Pastor Fritz enters the sanctuary. Frodo lies in the aisle between the pews, quietly nibbling on his paperclip.

A lot of the "churchy vocabulary" still used now finds its roots in Latin and Greek,

Worshippers in the sanctuary await the start of the service.

he explains. Sanctuary means "holy place," for example, and basilica refers to a rectangular room in historical Roman law courts. The nave, where the congregation sits, comes from the same root as navy, creating parallelism between today's congregations and the Roman method of sailing when oars were used in addition to sails. Rowers sat in rows, just as worshippers sit in rows of pews.

And then there are the stoles. Stoles come in vibrant colors, like Lutheran versions of the Japanese obi, the colored belts worn in martial arts. Each stole represents a different religious holiday or event. Pastor Fritz reaches into a closet and pulls out the end of each stole, attributing specific events to each color—green for normal Sundays, blue for Advent, violet for Lent, red for the Day of Pentecost. "Lutherans are historically visual and musical. These fabric strips and cords go over the clergy's shoulders and represent an artistic rendition of the oxen's yoke. It signifies that a pastor is the servant of the people."

27

Open and Inclusive
— University United Methodist Church,
East Lansing

By Katlin Barth with photography by Alyssa Kobylarek

"AS DISCIPLES OF Jesus Christ, we are an open and inclusive congregation and welcome all persons into full participation." University United Methodist Church congregants demonstrate that its hospitality statement is more than just a good line in its brochure. You might walk in as a stranger, but you won't remain one for long. Smiling faces greet worshippers as they walk toward the sanctuary. Each passing hand is shaken.

Senior Pastor Jennifer Browne describes her members as a warm congregation of people who are good at introducing themselves to newcomers. During the service, members help visitors find hymns in the hymnals and invite them back the following Sunday. Another example: after one service, a member who refers to herself as the shortest person present introduces herself to the tallest worshipper there, a freshman at Michigan State University. After a quick laugh about their height difference, she wishes him good luck in his studies.

The sanctuary fills with the voices of the choir and the worshippers.

Because Pastor Browne grew up nonreligious, she is familiar with what it feels like to arrive at a church alone and unknowing. "I'm way more attuned to what somebody without a church background might encounter. I know how intimidating it is to walk into a church by yourself and have no idea what's going on." Because of her personal experiences, she makes sure visitors aren't left to figure things out for themselves.

An impossible-to-miss information center is the first thing you see as you walk up the stairs to the main floor. Each visitor receives a letter detailing key facts about University United Methodist, a name tag and a form to request more information. A pamphlet with "The Lord's Prayer" explains the worship service. Although every member may know that prayer, Pastor Browne didn't as a new Christian, so she tries to make it easier for those starting their spiritual journeys to participate during the service.

Student visitors get an additional brochure about the Wesley Foundation, the campus ministry led by Pastor William Chu at Michigan State. The campus ministry also offers a more contemporary worship service. Participants gathers on Sundays at 5:30 p.m. to share a meal and discuss Scripture. On Thursdays at 8 p.m., members attend their own worship service called TGIT—Thank God It's Thursday—which includes a short sermon and contemporary music followed by drinks, snacks and socializing.

A stack of hymnals rests on a pew after the service concludes.

WALKING INTO THE sanctuary before the service, you see congregants turned in every direction chatting with those nearby. Students, families and older couples fill the pews. Pastor Browne says:

> *The people who come here like diversity. We have an international flavor. It's not over-whelming, but because we're on the campus we get a lot of international folks. Because of the open-minded theology of this congregation, we're tolerant of a lot of different kinds of lifestyles. We very much reflect the campus and the greater Lansing community.*

Jim Doyle has been attending University United Methodist since 1965. Asked by his son why he's always gone there, Doyle responds that it's because of the people. He also likes the many mission projects that give congregants opportunities to help others.

Sharing is the main topic of discussion during one Sunday service. Mark Doyal, the communications director for the Michigan Area of the United Methodist Church, says the church is "blessed with a congregation that focuses on missions in the community and worldwide." Everyone has something to give, he continues, whether it's singing in the choir, offering a smile or volunteering their time.

PASTOR BROWNE JOINED the clergy not only because she felt called by God to do so but also to share her talents. She laughs as she remembers her freshman year of college. She'd taken a career assessment test and being a priest, minister or rabbi was one of her top career matches. She posted the results on her dorm room door out of protest, not pride. "It was hilarious because I didn't believe in God," she says. Back then, she thought the test result was a fluke, but it proved to be right on target.

Pastor Browne found God during her senior year when she "had a visit from the Holy Spirit that changed the way I look at everything and changed my life." She joined the clergy in part due to her personal faith journey and in part because that's where God called her to be in the world. However, another part of the decision was a desire to use her skills to teach a congregation.

She hopes these congregants will do the same by using the gifts given to them by God to love God and their neighbors, and she says they should expect the same from her. She also wants the congregation to know that the leader isn't there to do the work for them. While she's more than willing to provide resources, the rest is in their own hands. "Being a part of a congregation is more about giving rather than receiving. It's about helping the world."

During worship, she tries to deliver a message that inspires congregants to get out of

Worshippers are asked to pray over the quilts and pass on their prayers to the people who will receive them.

their pews and help others. During one service, Kristen Dunn, the church's small group ministry coordinator, invites worshippers to contribute their time and talents and stop by her table later. As part of her job, Dunn organizes study fellowship groups that allow members to get to know each other on a deeper level than is possible on a busy Sunday morning.

There are almost 500 members, and while not everyone helps out in or out of the church, Pastor Browne says the majority do. "There is a flavor in this congregation where if you're a part of us, you should be doing something besides just coming on Sundays. You should find some way to serve," whether locally or internationally. "I'm proud to be a part of a congregation that does as much outreach as this church does."

For example, members create Thanksgiving baskets for neighbors in need. Members of the Ugly Quilts group use their sewing skills to make quilts for the homeless and for people who have moved into new homes and don't have warm blankets. Members also participate in a CROP Hunger Walk to raise money to feed the hungry in the East Lansing area.

Pastor Jennifer Browne hugs a worshipper. She takes time to get to know the congregants after each Sunday service.

To provide assistance beyond the United States, Doyal introduced a mission trip to Mizak, Haiti, to build the first health clinic to serve the mountainous community of 35,000 people. University United Methodist and other United Methodist churches in the state actively support many mission programs in that country, including Haitian Artisans for Peace International (HAPI).

PASTOR BROWNE FEELS called to move the church through the twenty-first century, and children and youth play an important role in that movement. The younger ages force the rest of us to change, she says. "We need to listen to young folks and ask them how they best hear the message of God and how to talk about things that aren't normally talked about." With an intergenerational group, University United Methodist bridges gaps between children in kindergarten and grandparents. Nowhere else in our culture do multiple generations encounter and engage one another as they do in churches, she says, and "each is enriched by broadening their mind to understand the other age group." Some congregants resist change because they want the church to be the same as it's always been, but she sees that attitude as more harmful than helpful.

The Sunday morning service bridges old and new ways of worship and appeals to those looking for traditional yet lively worship, such as that on Jazz Sundays. Music is embedded in the church's history, so guest musicians, including guitarists, saxophonists and drummers provide a strong, lively beat for the choir and congregation to sing and clap to.

As longtime parishioner Doyle says, "It's not always like this, but when it is, it's good."

The sanctuary where Sunday worship includes a sermon, Scripture readings, prayer, choral music and special musical guests.

ONE
COMMUNITY
ONE
WEEK
MANY
FAITHS

In Conclusion: All Religions Are One

By Eric Freedman

Early in the morning our song shall rise to you.
　　—From a Roman Catholic prayer

F OR MORE THAN six decades, the brick structure of the
Church of the Resurrection has stood about midway between the Michigan State University campus and the state Cap-
itol in downtown Lansing. The site's legacy is even older, almost
a century old, because Mass was first celebrated in its original
building there in 1922.

At an 8:15 a.m. Mass on a crisp mid-fall Tuesday, a priest
and his parishioners sing, *Holy, holy, holy, Lord God Almighty.*
Early in the morning our song shall rise to you. And song did
rise—song of praise, song of prayer, song of fealty, song of faith.
Our Father who art in heaven, hallowed be thy name, they intoned
in the familiar recitation of the Lord's Prayer. Parishioners wish

each other *Peace be with you*, shaking hands, occasionally hugging. And then they leave to pursue their day's activities.

We could read too much or too little into this tiny slice of the diverse faiths in our community. We could say the Church of the Resurrection symbolically, as well as physically, straddles two major parts of the community—the university and the downtown's government agencies and businesses. We also could say that because the church's Mass lasted only a half hour, religion plays only a small role in the day-to-day lives of its parishioners. Neither of these statements is demonstrably true or false. We don't know whether community residents see any symbolic significance in the physical location. We don't know how individual parishioners integrate faith and prayer into their own relationships and activities at work, at home, with neighbors and friends, with nonreligious organizations or public officials. What we do know is this: The Church of the Resurrection has long been a spiritual center in our community and a visible landmark to Catholics and non-Catholics alike.

As this book demonstrates, however, we also know it's not the only religious institution that is a visible landmark and a spiritual center in the Lansing area. Each house of worship that our writers and photographers visited for this project has a physical and spiritual presence. Each sees its roles in the community in multiple ways, just as each professes its beliefs through formal and informal worship in different ways.

This is the hour of change
Within it we stand uncertain on the border of light
Shall we draw back or cross over
Where shall our hearts turn
Shall we draw back, my brother, my sister, or cross over
　　—From the Sabbath readings in *Mishkan T'filah: A Reform Siddur*

THREE DAYS LATER and a few blocks from the Michigan State campus, my wife and I join about twenty students gathered in the living room of the Lester & Jewell Morris Hillel Jewish Student Center to light the *Shabbat* candles. The students then divide into two groups, some for a Conservative service in one room and the others—including us—for a Reform service in a small basement room with a Holy Ark and its eternal flame (*Ner Tamid* in Hebrew) and the flags of Israel and the United States of America.

This is a worship service of the students, by the students and for the students. No rabbi, no cantor and, except for my wife and me, no "adults." We aren't the only visitors: three first-year criminal justice students attend as well. Their purpose: a cultural immersion assignment for one of their courses.

The lay leader of the service, a business major at the university, plays his guitar. Most of the prayers are traditional and familiar from my childhood, but many of the melodies are not. As for the English translations in the *siddur* (prayer book), gone are the formal "thee" and "thy" I remember from childhood. They've been replaced by the more casual, conversational "you" and "your."

There is no sermon. Rather, there's an opportunity for all of us to state our names and tell about a *simcha* (joyful event) we'd experienced during the week. For several students, the *simcha* was the end of midterm exams.

Shout it out loud.
—From a prayer sung at First Assembly of God of Greater Lansing

ARMS STRETCH UPWARD in supplication, in prayer, in thanks. Hands are raised high and wave as a five-piece band plays and six members of a vocal team sing background vocals. A grandmother lovingly holds her 2-month-old grandchild, who sleeps through the jubilant, joyous enthusiasm sweeping through the sanctuary.

It's a bright Sunday morning at First Assembly of God of Greater Lansing, "a local church with an international focus" and congregants from twenty-nine countries. Among the worshippers this day are members of Teen Challenge, an Assemblies of God outreach mission that works with people with addictions and other "life-controlling problems."

October is "Pastor Appreciation Month," an event of higher-than-usual significance to this congregation because their pastor will undergo surgery in a few days. Thus this Sunday marks the start of forty days of prayer and fasting by congregants "to lift him up in prayer" for the operation and recovery.

Fittingly, the pastor's sermon this day is faith, a message accompanied by readings from Matthew, John and Hebrews and punctuated with "amen" and "hallelujah." How do we balance faith with reality? How does our individual reality change over time, especially as we age? We hear how his grandmother's reality, her real world, shrank when she moved into the Florida nursing home that she later came to cherish as her home. And we learn how the pastor's reality expanded when, after driving through New York's Adirondack Mountains into Vermont, he accidentally found the studio where the American folk artist Grandma Moses had worked.

Enrich the poor, raise the fallen, comfort the sorrowful, bring healing to the sick, reassure the fearful, rescue the oppressed, bring hope to the hopeless, shelter the destitute.

   —From "Strive," a Baha'i prayer

IT IS A celebration of the birthday of the Bab, the prophet-herald of the Baha'i Faith, a widely dispersed religion globally but little known by most Americans.

Unlike most of the other congregations in this book, members of the small Baha'i community in the Lansing area have no permanent building. Instead, they usually worship in each other's homes. But today is one of the Faith's nine annual holidays, so they gather in the recital hall of the East Lansing Hannah Community Center for music, worship, fellowship and food.

"God is one, man is one, and all religions are one," the opening song proclaims. As my wife and I wait for the service to start, we talk with others about the persecution of Baha'is, especially in Iran, where the Bab founded the faith in 1844 and where authorities arrested, assaulted, jailed and executed him in a public square six years later. We speak of our children, of the growth of the Faith through word of mouth rather than evangelism or proselytizing, of the Faith's pacifist beliefs and of its conviction that believers also must obey the laws of their own countries.

A law student from Iran plays traditional drums. A girl, the youngest child in the congregation that day, is called forward for a reading but shyly clings to her mother, then quietly whispers part of the prayer she would not read. Her older brother exhibits no such reluctance as he gives his reading.

———

I RECENTLY READ an article about diversity of community by syndicated newspaper columnist Connie Schultz. "Put fifty people—any fifty people—in a room and ask them what they think of God and you'll get fifty different stories about fifty different journeys," she writes. "At the beginning, it seemed the thing we had in common was a desire to talk about why we believe what we believe. By the end, though, it was clear that most wanted to figure out how to build community in a country that often feels inhabited by strangers."

But religious institutions are only part of the solution to building community in contemporary America. As Schultz observes, "There was a time when houses of worship filled the gap as conveners of diverse populations. Like many baby boomers, I remember when bankers, welders, teachers and cashiers sat in the same pews. They knew one another's names. That's changed now."

That's changed in the Lansing area as well. We who work and live here are often divided and simultaneously torn in multiple directions by our busy electronics-driven lives, with malls, with parks, with hundreds of cable and satellite channels, with crowded school curricula, with polarized partisan politics, with worries about unemployment and about budget-challenged public services.

So is there a role in community-building for the area's 400-plus houses of worship, and if so, what is that role? Or it may be more accurate to ask what are their roles, plural? Our authors and photographers provide insights for answering those questions.

What did our authors and photographers discover during this project? Unexpected joys, the warmth of a stranger's welcome, diversity of people and beliefs and cultures and languages, the thought-provoking nature of silence, physical manifestations of faith and invisible manifestations of faith, generosity, sorrow at seeing congregations age toward death, the energy of congregations young and exuberant, families together, art. They discovered true believers and seekers. They found people for whom organized religion is a cornerstone of daily life and those for whom it's primarily social and not spiritual. They discovered that service can be equally valid and equally satisfying whether it's within the four walls of a sanctuary or in the streets and schools of their neighborhoods.

And they discovered valuable things about themselves.

Amen.

Editors and Contributors

EDITORS

ERIC FREEDMAN is a Pulitzer Prize-winning journalist, Knight Chair and director of the Knight Center for Environmental Journalism at Michigan State University. He is a former associate dean of International Studies & Programs and a former Fulbright Scholar in Uzbekistan and Lithuania. His previous books include *Presidents and Black America: A Documentary History* and *After the Czars and Commissars: Journalism in Authoritarian Post-Soviet Central Asia*.

HOWARD BOSSEN is professor of photography and visual communication in the School of Journalism at Michigan State University and adjunct curator of photography at the Michigan State University Museum. He is the author the books *Henry Holmes Smith: Man of Light* and *Luke Swank: Modernist Photographer*. Bossen was a Distinguished Visiting Professor in the Center for the Arts in Society at Carnegie Mellon University in 2002 and a Fulbright-Robles Senior Scholar in Mexico in the mid-1990s.

PREFACE

SUE CARTER is a professor of journalism at Michigan State University and rector of St. John's Episcopal Church in Howell, Michigan.

WRITERS

JOSH ANDERSON is a sophomore in Professional Writing with a minor in Japanese. He is from Aurora, Illinois.

KATLIN BARTH graduated in 2014 with a bachelor's degree in Journalism. She is from Ida, Michigan.

LEAH BENOIT graduated in 2014 with bachelor's degrees in Communication and Journalism with a specialization in Public Relations. She is from Royal Oak, Michigan.

MARISA HAMEL is a junior in Journalism and Social Relations & Policy. She is from Syracuse, New York.

TYLER HENDON graduated in 2014 with a bachelor's degree in Journalism. He is from Ferndale, Michigan.

JORDAN JENNINGS is a junior in Photojournalism and Spanish. She is from Perry, Michigan.

DUYGU KANVER is a doctoral student in Media and Information Studies. She is from Istanbul, Turkey.

YVONNE MAKIDON graduated in 2013 with a Ph.D. in Human Development & Family Studies. She is from Flushing, Michigan.

RJ WOLCOTT graduated in 2014 with a bachelor's degree in Journalism with a specialization in Editorial Reporting. He is from Spring Lake, Michigan.

Editors and Contributors

PHOTOGRAPHERS

BREANNA BISHOP graduated in 2014 with a bachelor's degree in Journalism. She is from Detroit, Michigan.

ERIN HAMPTON is a senior in Journalism with a specialization in Design. She is from West Bloomfield, Michigan.

OLIVIA HILL is a senior in Professional Writing. She is from Royal Oak, Michigan.

BRITTANY HOLMES graduated in 2013 with a bachelor's degree in Media Arts & Technology, with a specialization in TV, Cinema & Radio and a cognate in Social Science. She is from Grand Rapids, Michigan.

ELIZABETH IZZO is a junior in Creative Advertising. She is from New Berlin, Wisconsin.

JORDAN JENNINGS is a junior in Photojournalism and Spanish. She is from Perry, Michigan.

ALYSSA KOBYLAREK graduated in 2014 with a bachelor's degree in Journalism. She is from Novi, Michigan.

CARRA OTETO is a junior in Journalism. She is from Grand Rapids, Michigan.

ANDREA RABY is a senior in Journalism. She is from Grand Rapids, Michigan.

DYLAN SOWLE graduated in 2014 with a bachelor's degree in Journalism. He is from Grand Ledge, Michigan.

KATIE STIEFEL is a junior in Journalism. She is from South Lyon, Michigan.

ASHLEY WEIGEL is a senior in Journalism and Media & Information. She is from Ann Arbor, Michigan.

DESIGNER

KENNETH VILLAPANDO graduated in 2014 with a bachelor's degree in Telecommunication, Information Studies & Media with a specialization in Creative Advertising. He is from Auburn Hills, Michigan.

COPY EDITORS

ERICA GOLDMAN graduated in 2014 with a bachelor's degree in Professional Writing. She is from Novi, Michigan.

RACHAEL LEFEVRE is a senior in Professional Writing. She is from Kalamazoo, Michigan.

CAROLINE WHITE is a junior in English and Professional Writing. She is from Stockbridge, Michigan.

MARKETER

NICOLE WEBER graduated in 2014 with a bachelor's degree in Professional Writing. She is from Lansing, Michigan.